# Sunshine Cuisine

# Sunshine Cuisine

**JEAN-PIERRE BREHIER**

WITH FELICIA GRESSETTE

HEARST BOOKS
NEW YORK

It is the policy of William Morrow and Company, Inc., and its
imprints and affiliates, recognizing the importance of preserving
what has been written, to print the books we publish on acid-free
paper, and we exert our best efforts to that end.

Library of Congress Cataloging-in-Publication Data

Brehier, Jean-Pierre.
    Sunshine cuisine / Jean-Pierre Brehier with Felicia Gres-
sette.
            p.          cm.
        Includes index.
        ISBN 0–688–13118–2
        1. Cookery.   I. Gressette, Felicia.   II. Title.
    TX714.B74   1994
    641.5—dc20                                      93–24404
                                                        CIP

Printed in the United States of America

First Edition

1   2   3   4   5   6   7   8   9   10

BOOK DESIGN AND ILLUSTRATIONS BY RICHARD ORIOLO

Pour Maman
qui est la source
de mon inspiration

# *Acknowledgments*

*I* have so many people to thank, so many wonderful friends who believed in me from the very beginning. And with their faith and support, I was able to make this book a reality.

First and foremost, I want to thank the entire team at WPBT, Channel 2, in Miami. Enormous thanks and gratitude go to Barry Chase, the show's executive producer, for the vision to create *Sunshine Cuisine* and the leadership to see it through; to Angel Hernandez, director of production, for all his wonderful advice; to Joe Jabaly, producer, for allowing me to be me; and to Richard Carpenter, director, for being so excellent at his job.

I also want to thank the camera operators, Clare, Art, Alfred, and Will, for their fantastic work, and Kiki, our floor manager, who kept us all smiling and happy. Thanks also to Joe Saitta, who designed a beautiful set; Tony, our lighting designer; Rick on audio; and Diane in makeup. I am particularly grateful to Kevin, Jerry, Bob, and Hans, my kitchen assistants, for contributing their time and culinary talents.

I feel a deep sense of gratitude to Al Marchioni, president and CEO of William Morrow, and Ann Bramson, my editor, for their vote of confidence in this book. I am equally indebted to my agents, Eric and Maureen Lasher, for believing in *Sunshine Cuisine* before anyone else. Thank you for your continued guidance.

This book would not have existed without the help of Darlene, my secretary, and Felicia, my co-writer. Thank you, Darlene, for working endless hours, never complaining and always with a smile. Thank you for keeping my recipes organized and for helping me find just the right word. Thank you, Felicia, for having faith in this book from the beginning. Thank you for your friendship and diligent recipe testing.

I also want to thank my entire team at The Left Bank Restaurant: My chefs, Jacky, Bradley, Deborah, and Johnny, who helped in the development and preparation of many recipes, and my dining room staff for keeping the restaurant's high standards. To all my loyal customers, thank you so much for your continued patronage, kind praise, and enthusiastic support for my many projects!

To Doug Castanedo, my photographer, for your friendship, talent, and patience.

To Dick Cingolani, for being such a great comrade, fellow chef, and humanitarian.

To Ed, my dear friend, for allowing me to find more energy when I thought I had none left.

To Steve Kane and Lew Krone at Fort Lauderdale radio station WFTL for supporting me and giving me an opportunity to do my radio show.

And, thank you, again, from the bottom of my heart, to all my friends, business associates, customers, readers, and listeners for believing in me!

*Contents*

# Preface

You may be wondering just what Sunshine Cuisine is. Well, I live in Florida, so that should be a hint. And I grew up in the south of France—there's another clue.

Actually, Sunshine Cuisine is a style of cooking that relies on classical techniques and uses ingredients that are full-flavored, tropical, and Mediterranean in style and influence. It combines the taste memories of my childhood in Provence with the Florida-Caribbean influences that have shaped my professional career as a chef.

Sunshine Cuisine is food that is unpretentious, with bright, strong flavors—olive oil, fresh herbs, grilled seafood, tomatoes, garlic, citrus, papaya, and mango—and all the fresh ingredients that are the signature of Mediterranean and Caribbean cooking.

This book also gives you the why, as well as the how, of the kitchen. Recipes are written in such vivid detail that even novice cooks, making a simple sauce, can almost hear the sizzle of wine splashed into a hot sauté pan and inhale the unmistakable aroma of crushed garlic as it releases its fragrance.

Sunshine Cuisine is both down to earth and creative. And it's delicious!

# Introduction

$I$t all started about thirty-five years ago, the first time I made fresh pasta with my grandmother. I was five years old and growing up in a small town in the south of France. I can still remember standing on a wooden crate so I could work next to Grandmère on her big, white marble-top kitchen counter. With more flour on my face and in my hair than in the pasta, I was having the time of my life!

Food was my grandmother's whole life, after her family. She raised rabbits, chickens, geese, ducks, and even had a goat to make homemade goat cheese. The second you opened the kitchen door to the garden, you could smell the pungent aroma of the four kinds of tomatoes she grew. In her half-acre garden, she raised and harvested cauliflower, zucchini, egg-plant, cucumbers, and potatoes. When she wasn't cooking or baking, she was tending her garden or her animals. I can still hear her saying, "Feed this goose a little more than the other; it's the one we are going to eat for Christmas!"

Growing up in the country taught me how pure, natural, and fresh ingredients should taste. Those special times of love and creating in my grandmother's kitchen gave me the joy of cooking that I possess to this day.

I lived with my parents, two sisters, Beatrice and Genevieve, and my brother Bernard (also brother Pascal who came along ten years later) in a little town called Le Tolonet, ten miles from Aix-en-Provence and at the foot of Mont Saint Victoire, which Paul Cézanne painted so many times. The air smelled of fragrant lavender, fresh thyme, and sweet basil. Our home was on top of a hill covered with thousands of wild flowers in all shapes and colors.

Olive, apple, and cherry trees gave us shade from the hot summer sun and fruit for our table. The cherries were large and deep red; their flavor, in my memory, was incredibly intense. I couldn't wait for them to ripen so we could pick them and bring them home for my mother to make cherry cobbler with hand-churned vanilla-bean ice cream or her famous cherry clafoutis. I have shared both recipes with you in this book.

My mother, who is Italian, taught us to use vegetables, herbs, and fruit when they are at their peak of flavor. She treated ingredients with respect; and that is probably the most important culinary lesson that I ever learned! It is the foundation of my cooking to this day.

Some of my best memories are of spending Sundays with my mother at the local open-air market. In France, farmers bring their beautiful fruits and vegetables every other day to the town center, which is closed to traffic. Among the wares displayed are forty or fifty kinds of olives, from tiny green to huge black ones, all bobbing in fifty-gallon casks; tons of garlic bulbs, all different shapes and sizes; live chickens, roosters, ducks, geese, and quail as well as dozens of eggs, ranging from tiny to fist size, from pale cream to rich brown in color; and because this is France, flower vendors arrange their beautiful wares by the bunch in tall galvanized-tin pails. After all, how can you have a table without flowers?

Every merchant has the same location week after week, and sellers and buyers come to know each other. It's like one big party! Lots of talk. That was the only part I didn't like about shopping with my mother. She loved to talk!

After a couple of hours, we had bought everything we needed, placed the food in our net shopping bags, and walked home. Then we would spend the rest of the morning cooking the day's meals.

You should have seen the way my mother would orchestrate the meal. I was amazed that somehow each dish would be ready just on time. While a fluffy white chocolate mousse was chilling in the refrigerator, a veal roast would be slowly cooking along with a dozen different vegetables all cut and shaped perfectly and everyone at the table was already enjoying a beautiful cheese soufflé.

Growing up in a household that revolved around food, it's no wonder that my first real job involved cooking. When I was twelve years old I spent an entire summer working for my uncle René, a pastry chef and master bread maker, in his bakery. Starting at 3:00 A.M., my job was to shape the long French baguettes and make five slashes in each one with a razor blade. This procedure is very important in French bread making because it allows the dough to swell as the bread is baking. When Uncle René made the slashes, his hand would flash in what looked like a single, swift motion. The process was more painstaking for me, but after a few months I became almost as fast as my uncle.

He would also let me arrange the fruit on fresh strawberry tarts and, using a paint brush, I would coat them with apricot glaze. I loved working with Uncle René; he was a good teacher. I vividly remember watching him feed his huge, wood-burning oven to bake hundreds of baguettes. He would use different sizes of flat wooden spatulas—some eight to ten feet long— to insert and remove the bread from the oven. His ease and expertise fascinated me.

My first experience in a commercial kitchen was when I worked in the basement of a butcher shop that specialized in sausages. Starting at six in the morning, I would open up the sausage casings, which had been soaking in formaldehyde, attach them to an old-fashioned crank machine, and begin hours of sausage making. You would think this unglamorous task would discourage anyone from cooking professionally. But as much as I hated the smell of the formaldehyde, I loved the finished product— beautiful duck, lamb, pheasant, or wild-boar sausages with all kinds of wonderful seasonings.

On my fourteenth birthday, I went to work in a small, exquisite restaurant called L'Orangerie in Aix-en-Provence. The chef, Michel Moulin, took me under his wing and shared his lifetime of experience with me. He could tell, without looking in the oven, just from the aroma in the kitchen, that there were ducks cooking and that they were done. Or he would look at a stew and, without touching it, tell exactly how much longer it should be cooked. I marveled at his ability to extract maximum flavor from any ingredient he worked with, from a sprig of rosemary to a whole pig. He just knew how to cook.

I learned the fundamentals from this talented, generous man, and I went on to work in some of the best restaurants in the south of France, including Le Vendôme in Aix-en-Provence and L'Oustaù de Baumanière in Les Baux-de-Provence. Each restaurant taught me something different. Each chef had a different vision of how food should be served and paired with other foods.

All of these chefs, like my mother and grandmother, had respect for the traditions of the French kitchen. They would always refer to food history and the writings of famous chefs like Escoffier and Brillat-Savarin, the founders of today's classic French cuisine.

A stretch cooking aboard a French cruise liner in the Caribbean was my introduction to tropical fish, fruit, and produce, which were bought in port and then cooked in the traditional French style.

I came to America in 1973 and got a job at a Fort Lauderdale restaurant called Le Dôme, which served classic French cuisine and offered white-glove service. The manager, who conducted my job interview in French (I spoke no English), knew of the places I had worked in France and hired me. I was excited to be working in the best French restaurant in town. Right up my alley!

To make a good impression on my first day, I arrived early and checked in with the chef. What hadn't entered my mind was that the entire kitchen staff was American and no one spoke a word of French. Needless to say, my first night at Le Dôme was a total fiasco! I had no idea what anyone was talking about.

The next day I was washing dishes in a small Spanish restaurant, where I would soon learn English and become the chef.

In two years' time, I became the proud owner of a small Fort Lauderdale restaurant, which was a fondue place at that time. The restaurant had a guitarist and a very heavy bar business. There was no dress code; everyone wore shorts, flip-flops, and tank tops. The most expensive item on the menu was $6.95. If I prepared a daily special at $7.25, it wouldn't sell.

Converting the menu to classic French cuisine wasn't easy, but after a name change and some remodeling, two years later The Left Bank restaurant was voted one of the best restaurants in Fort Lauderdale. And seventeen years later, it is still ranked one of Florida's one hundred best restaurants.

Now I have directed my energies into this book and my new television cooking show, and I am happy to share with you many of the recipes I have been preparing through the years. I sincerely hope you will enjoy cooking from this book as much as I have enjoyed writing it for you. Each recipe has been tested, but be sure to read everything very carefully before you begin.

*Happy cooking.*

# Notes on Ingredients, Equipment, and Cooking Techniques

*M*y goal in life is to teach as many people as possible how to cook. And I hope that through this book, I can inspire confidence among hobbyist cooks so that they will feel comfortable enough to tackle any recipe.

I have been fortunate to work in some of the best restaurants in the world, and with some incredible chefs, one of whom was my mother. In my twenty-six years of experience in the restaurant business, I have observed one trait shared by all of the great chefs. All respected the ingredients that they were using.

I know that may sound perplexing. How exactly do you respect a tomato? First, make sure that you buy a good tomato, one that was left to ripen on the vine. It will be more fruity and less acidic than a tomato that was picked green. You should not refrigerate ripening tomatoes, as it will interfere with their flavor. If you are going to cook the tomatoes, take the skin off because it will become tough and chewy during cooking; the seeds will harden and become unpleasant to the bite.

Without giving you a complete lesson on the tomato, I am trying to illustrate the principles of respecting ingredients, of learning about the products you are working with, and of knowing how to buy, store and prepare them so you can extract the most flavor out of them. Always buy the freshest products and the best ingredients available.

As you read through the book and select recipes, be sure to read each one from top to bottom so that you have a good idea of what you should prepare ahead of time. This brings me to a very important point. Before you start any recipe, have everything ready and measured in advance. If the recipe calls for ½ cup chopped onion and 1 cup peeled, seeded, and chopped tomatoes, do not start to sauté the onion before preparing the tomatoes. If you do, the onion will be caramelized by the time you finish working with the tomatoes.

One of the most important lessons I have learned in cooking is that having everything cut and measured in advance is half the work. As you start your preparations, you may discover that you need to substitute certain ingredients that are not available. Do this with caution, especially the first time you prepare the recipe! If you cannot find fresh herbs, it's okay to use dried ones, but be sure to adjust the quantity, as you need less dried herbs than fresh. If you do not have the time to soak dried beans, you can use canned beans. Even though there is no excuse for not making your own stocks (since they are so easy to make), there are some decent canned products in your grocery store. But be careful and experiment with them, since some of them are very salty.

## Ingredients

### Oils

**OLIVE OIL:** Sometimes my recipes specify "extra-virgin olive oil," and sometimes just "olive oil." Maybe you are not sure of the difference. Extra-virgin olive oil is intensely fruity and fragrant and, in my opinion, should not be cooked. Heat destroys its fine and very special fruity character. So, I use it to complement salads or add personality to certain dishes. The term "extra-virgin" on the label means that the oil meets standards of low acidity (up to 1 percent) and comes from the first press of the olives. "First press," also called "cold pressed," means that the olives were crushed with cold stones made out of granite, which is the only stone that retains the cold. It's the super-premium variety.

"Pure olive oil," or "100 percent pure olive oil," on the other hand, is less delicate than extra-virgin and comes from a second or third pressing of the olives. Use it for cooking and many marinades. It's less expensive.

Buy olive oil in the size bottle that is appropriate for the amounts that you use. Don't buy a gallon if it will take you a year to use it, since the oil can develop a rancid taste. Keep olive oil in a cool, dark place, but don't refrigerate it if you can help it. Olive oil will grow thick and cloudy in the refrigerator; let it come to room temperature and it will "melt."

**SUNFLOWER OIL:** This is the vegetable oil I prefer for sautéing, and for all other preparations that don't require the stronger taste of olive oil. Sunflower oil has a mild, buttery taste that I find appealing.

**PEANUT OIL:** The peanut oil I knew as a child had a beautiful roasted peanut flavor, like Chinese peanut oil. The kind sold in supermarkets is practically tasteless. However, it is great to use when making flavored oil, as it will not interfere with the aroma and taste of the herb or spice that you are trying to capture.

**GRAPE-SEED OIL:** This oil is a by-product of wine making, made by squeezing whatever is left over after the grapes are crushed. You would think that this oil has a great fruity flavor. Quite the contrary, it is lighter than peanut and sunflower oils. It, too, is excellent to use in making flavored oil.

## Vinegars

In *Sunshine Cuisine,* you'll see that I use a variety of vinegars in marinades, vinaigrettes, and sauces. It is important to choose the right vinegar for the recipe.

**SHERRY WINE VINEGAR:** Made from sherry, it has a rich and very aromatic, distinctive taste. It is often used on salads or to enhance a delicate sauce.

**WHITE WINE VINEGAR:** Mild and pale straw-colored, this vinegar adds flavor but not color (as red wine vinegar does). I use it a great deal in my cooking. A good chardonnay vinegar or a good Champagne vinegar has finesse and lends a soft, delicate flavor to food.

**RICE WINE VINEGAR:** Very mild and light, usually clear in color, use it when you only want a hint of vinegar. Great to perk up a sauce that fell asleep and needs a shot of personality.

**RED WINE VINEGAR:** Stronger and red in color; use it with robust ingredients, such as garlic and olive oil. Buy the best quality available. A red vinegar from the French Bordeaux region will have similar characteristics to a red Bordeaux wine.

**APPLE CIDER VINEGAR:** When of superior quality, it has a beautiful apple flavor. Mild and very good for light-flavored marinades, apple cider vinegar is also low in acidity.

**BALSAMIC VINEGAR:** A vinegar that is allowed to age a minimum of four years in huge oak or chestnut barrels. Some of the finest balsamic vinegars are aged for twenty to fifty years and become more like a condiment that adds a pungent sweetness to dishes. You can even drizzle balsamic vinegar on strawberries. Always buy the best you can afford—in a gourmet food shop, not in the supermarket or grocery store. And remember, the better the quality, the less you need to use.

## Wine and Spirits

We use a lot of wine and spirits in the kitchen because they add so much flavor to food. Not only do we cook with red and white wines, vermouth, and sherry, we also frequently use port wine in sauces because of its characteristic robust, fruity flavor.

It's not necessary to buy very expensive wines to use in cooking, but be sure they are good enough for you to drink. The flavor won't get any better in cooking. My mother had a great philosophy, "If you can't drink it, then you can't cook with it." Stay away from salted cooking wines.

## Herbs

The Left Bank has an herb garden that provides the many fresh herbs we use in our cooking. Of course, you can buy fresh herbs in many supermarkets, but why not try growing a few yourself? They're easy to grow as long as they get lots of sunshine, a well-drained soil, and a drink of water when they need it.

We use a lot of cilantro, or fresh coriander, which has a distinctive and pungent taste. Some people love it (I do!), while others don't care for it at all.

I recommend that you grow basil, for making pesto and for an intense flavor that marries so well with tomatoes. Also, thyme, with its tiny leaves, and rosemary, for its resinous, lemonlike aroma, are wonderful for marinades and partner very well with pork and veal.

# Eggs

We have included several recipes in *Sunshine Cuisine* that use raw eggs—classics, such as mayonnaise, and new creations, such as Citron Mousse—although some health authorities advise against eating uncooked eggs because of the slight risk of salmonella. For safety's sake, buy eggs from a reliable source and check that the shells are intact.

# Dairy

We've cut down on the amounts of butter and cream in many of the recipes in *Sunshine Cuisine,* but sometimes there's no substitute for the fresh, creamy taste of dairy products.

Always use unsalted butter in your cooking; it's fresher and tastes cleaner (salt is used as a preservative). It makes more sense to add salt to taste than to use salted butter.

**CRÈME FRAÎCHE:** A tangy, nutty-tasting, slightly fermented version of heavy cream that you can buy in specialty food stores or make at home. It's easy to make. Just make sure to buy heavy cream that has been pasteurized but not ultrapasteurized.

**GOAT CHEESE:** I love the tangy smoothness of a mild, fresh goat cheese. Both domestic and imported French goat cheese are available in supermarkets. Freshly made, it is much milder than the somewhat chalky French version.

**PARMESAN CHEESE:** I am partial to Parmigiano-Reggiano, the smoothest yet most flavorful of all the Parmesan cheeses and available in most well-stocked markets. The cheese is left to age two to three years. Do not even consider buying an already grated cheese.

**MOZZARELLA:** There is no substitute for fresh buffalo mozzarella, a soft white cheese, originally made with buffalo's milk, served with vine-ripened tomatoes and a basil and balsamic vinaigrette. Nowadays most cheese makers make mozzarella from cow's milk. Sometimes you can find fresh Italian buffalo mozzarella in high-quality gourmet shops or Italian specialty stores.

## Olives

The strong, tangy flavor of Mediterranean olives is essential to *Sunshine Cuisine*. I love the briny, dark Calamata olives from Greece and the smaller, wrinkled, oil-cured Niçoise olives from France. Green olives from California are fine, but stay away from the bland canned "ripe olives" found in the grocery store.

## Garlic

Do not even think about buying chopped garlic in oil. It's tasteless! Look for whole heads of garlic with tight, papery skin and firm cloves. Sometimes you will find a green center when you cut into a garlic clove; it is bitter-tasting, so remove it. A new crop of garlic (the California harvest is in the spring) is wonderful. As the year wears on, it becomes harder to find great garlic.

The easiest way to peel and crush garlic cloves is to use a large chef's knife. Put the garlic cloves on a cutting board, lay the flat side of the knife over a couple of cloves at a time. Hold the knife with one hand, make a fist with the other, and bang once or twice. The papery skin will slip off, then you can crush the garlic with the flat of the knife. If you need a lot of peeled, crushed garlic, separate the cloves from a whole head, wrap them in a kitchen towel, and bang them with a small, heavy frying pan.

## Tropical Fruits

Mangoes and papayas, as well as pineapples and citrus, are staples of the Sunshine Cuisine kitchen. They're widely available across the country, but you can always substitute peaches or nectarines for mangoes or papayas.

## Fresh Chili Peppers

My favorite fresh chili peppers give flavor as well as heat in marinades, salad dressings, and here and there in other recipes. I like habaneros and

Scotch Bonnets for their intense, fruity flavor and their hotness. I also love pimientos, Anaheim chilies, and jalapeño peppers. Most peppers can substitute for each other, so don't worry if the supply in your area is limited to jalapeños.

Remember that the heat of fresh chili peppers comes from the ribs and the seeds, so you can temper the intensity by discarding the seeds. I advise wearing rubber gloves when working with hot chilies. In any case, wash your hands thoroughly after cutting chilies and keep your fingers away from your eyes!

## Equipment

My kitchen is no stranger to gadgets, but you can make everything in this book with just a good knife and a blender. Here are a few additional kitchen toys to consider.

**IMMERSION BLENDER:** This great gadget is a hand held electric wand. Insert it into a saucepan, turn it on, and it purées soups and sauces right in the pan. Prices start at about $20, on sale.

**JUICER:** I use my juicer to make all kinds of combinations for sauces at The Left Bank. You can spend as little as $30 or as much as $200 on a juicer. Just be sure to choose one that is easy to clean.

**MANDOLINE:** Not a musical instrument, but a slicer, a mandoline is a long, narrow board with a razor-sharp blade insert. With it you can make very thin slices of potatoes, cucumbers, or other vegetables. It is extremely sharp, so be careful of your fingers. A serviceable plastic mandoline can cost as little as $30, or you can spend $120 for a professional-quality, stainless steel mandoline.

**FOOD PROCESSOR:** I have a medium-size processor (about 11 cups), and it's fine for home use. I also have a mini-processor that's good for chopping small quantities of fresh herbs, garlic, shallots, and so forth. A coffee grinder is great for pulverizing cinnamon, nutmeg, and nuts.

**TONGS:** Spring-loaded metal tongs are a chef's best friend, and it's amazing that more home cooks haven't discovered them. Using tongs is like extending the reach of your arm by about a foot. Tongs are great for sautéing and grilling because you can pick up food and turn it without poking a hole in it. Get some; they are inexpensive.

**WHISK:** Good for making sabayon, hollandaise, and mayonnaise. Make sure to buy a quality whisk, as it should last you a lifetime if you take good care of it.

**DOUBLE BOILER:** The bottom of the pot holds simmering water, the top holds food. A double boiler is essential for making egg sauces such as hollandaise and sabayon. It produces a very soft and even heat that allows eggs to cook but without becoming scrambled. A double boiler is also useful for making custards and for melting chocolate.

**SIEVES:** Get a couple of sizes to strain various mixtures. Choose different diameters and sizes of netting. The coarse netting is for the first straining of a stock, the finer netting for a delicate sauce or beurre blanc.

**GRILL:** We cook over hardwood charcoal at The Left Bank, and these recipes were tested on a charcoal grill. If yours is a gas-fired grill, that will work fine, too.

**OVENPROOF SAUTÉ PAN OR ROASTER:** I like to brown foods on one side on top of the stove, then turn them over and finish the cooking in the oven. For that, you need an all-metal sauté pan that can take the heat of the oven, or a roasting pan that can be used on a stovetop burner.

**PEPPER MILL:** You may think it's too much to own two pepper mills, but do yourself a great favor and go out and buy two very different-looking mills, one for black pepper and one for white pepper. The flavor and intensity of freshly ground pepper is much superior to the preground pepper available at the supermarket. Having two pepper mills allows you to have white pepper handy when a recipe calls for a milder pepper flavor or for when you prepare a light-colored sauce where you don't want specks of black pepper to stand out.

**CHEESE GRATER:** All you need is a simple inexpensive cheese grater so that you can grate fresh Parmesan on top of steaming buttered noodles, risotto, or a freshly tossed Caesar salad just before serving. And I promise that you will never go back to pregrated cheese in the box!

# Cooking Techniques

There are a few restaurant terms and techniques used extensively in *Sunshine Cuisine* that you may not recognize.

**PAN ROASTING:** I pan roast fish, veal chops, pork tenderloin, just about everything. It's easy. You just heat an ovenproof sauté pan on the stovetop, add the food and brown it on one side over moderately high heat, then turn the food over and place the pan in the oven to finish cooking. This produces juicy, flavorful results.

**EMULSIFIED VINAIGRETTE:** In this very simple procedure, all you do is place all the ingredients into the blender so that they will mix together to create a creamy, emulsified vinaigrette.

**REDUCING:** This is really evaporation! You bring a mixture to a boil, then lower the heat a bit, and let it bubble away until the volume has reduced by one third, or half, or whatever the recipe specifies. The water goes up in steam, leaving the flavor behind in an intensified version.

Reducing a mixture is a standard technique for making sauces. However, don't get carried away. After a while, the flavor vanishes into the air and is replaced by a caramelized and burned taste.

**BRAISING:** This term usually refers to meat or fish that is first seared in oil or butter, then cooked in stock or juices.

**COULIS:** This is a thick purée of vegetables or fruit that is mixed with stock or liquor for extra flavor.

**DEGLAZING:** This is done to dissolve the food particles that stick to the bottom of the roasting pan or sauté pan. Simply add wine, stock or water to the pan and stir over heat.

**EMULSION:** This is a mixture of two liquids that normally don't mix, such as oil and water. You make an emulsion, mayonnaise or hollandaise, by very gradually beating drops of one liquid, such as oil, into another, such as vinegar, so that the mixture becomes thick and shiny.

**JULIENNE:** This term refers to vegetables or fruit, cut into thin matchstick-size strips.

**SEARING:** Usually done in a sauté or roasting pan to capture all moisture inside the fish or meat. You heat oil or butter until very hot, then brown the meat or fish on all sides.

## Peeled, Seeded, and Chopped Tomatoes

The most efficient way to peel, seed, and chop a tomato is to slash an X on the bottom, briefly immerse the tomato in boiling water, then plunge it into ice water to stop the cooking. The peel will slip off easily. Then, cut the tomato in half crosswise and gently squeeze to remove the seeds. Finally, chop.

If you need only a small amount, it's easy to peel the tomato with a sharp vegetable peeler. Use a sawing motion to remove the skin.

# Appetizers

Wild Mushroom and Corn Fricassee

Grilled Shrimp with Chervil
Butter Sauce

Shrimp Taco with Coconut Curry Sauce

Shrimp Sambuca

Grilled Scallops with Yellow Bell Pepper–
Black Bean Salsa

Sautéed Scallops Tequila

Crabmeat Crepes

Sliced Duck Breast with Banana–Citrus
Vinaigrette

Garlic Crostini

Mozzarella, Tomato, and
Basil Crostini

Prosciutto, Leek, and Goat
Cheese Crostini

# Wild Mushroom and Corn Fricassee

*This very easy and quick recipe is very impressive-looking. The contrast in texture between the mushrooms and the corn makes this dish interesting. You can serve it as an appetizer with Garlic Crostini (page 31) or as a side dish.*

**MAKES 4 SERVINGS**

3 ears yellow corn, husks and
　silks removed
1 tablespoon olive oil
2 shallots, finely minced
2 tablespoons red wine vinegar
1 pound mixed wild and button
　mushrooms
1 teaspoon chopped fresh thyme
　leaves

1 teaspoon chopped fresh oregano
　leaves
1 cup peeled, seeded, and chopped
　tomatoes
Salt and freshly ground black
　pepper

Cook the corn in boiling, lightly salted water for 5 minutes. Drain and let cool briefly, then cut off kernels with a sharp knife and reserve.

In a sauté pan, heat the oil, add the shallots, and cook for 1 minute, then add the vinegar and raise the temperature to high. Let the vinegar bubble madly for 1 minute, then add the mushrooms and sauté quickly over high heat for about 2 minutes.

Add the corn, thyme, oregano, and tomatoes and toss just until mushrooms are warmed all the way through. Add salt and pepper to taste.

Serve immediately.

# Grilled Shrimp
## WITH CHERVIL BUTTER SAUCE

*This rich, tangy sauce is a garlic lover's dream. If you're worried about using sixteen whole cloves of garlic, blanching them in boiling water will remove any bitterness or sharpness. You could serve this sauce with broiled or sautéed shrimp, too. If chervil is hard to find, substitute Italian parsley or basil.*

**MAKES 4 SERVINGS**

2 pounds jumbo shrimp
   (about 15 per pound)

**MARINADE**
1 cup olive oil
4 minced garlic cloves
¼ cup fresh lemon juice
12 whole black peppercorns
1 bay leaf

**CHERVIL BUTTER SAUCE**
16 whole garlic cloves, unpeeled
1 tablespoon olive oil
3 tablespoons unsalted butter,
   divided
2 tablespoons lemon juice
½ cup Chardonnay or full-bodied
   dry white wine
2 tablespoons chopped fresh
   chervil
Salt and freshly ground black
   pepper to taste

*Marinate the shrimp:* Wash, peel, and devein the shrimp. Place in a glass bowl. Combine the marinade ingredients and pour over the shrimp. Let stand 1 hour at room temperature or cover and refrigerate for a minimum of 3 hours.

*Make the sauce:* Bring 2 cups of water to a boil in a stainless steel pan. Add the garlic cloves and let boil for 5 to 10 minutes. Drain in a colander. Fill the pot with water and repeat the process, cooking for 5 more minutes. Drain again.

Squeeze the papery skins and the cooked garlic cloves will pop out. Slice the cloves very thinly, lengthwise.

In a saucepan, heat the olive oil and 1 tablespoon of the butter. Lightly sauté the garlic until a light golden brown; do not burn. Add the lemon juice and the Chardonnay, and let bubble until volume is reduced by half.

Remove from heat and add the chopped chervil and the remaining butter, 1 tablespoon at a time. Add salt and pepper, and keep the sauce in a warm place while grilling the shrimp.

*Cook the shrimp:* Remove from marinade and grill over a medium fire for about 3 minutes on each side, just until opaque all the way through. Do not overcook.

Arrange on a platter and pour Chervil Butter Sauce over the shrimp.

# Shrimp Taco

## WITH COCONUT CURRY SAUCE

*T*his is, without a doubt, one of the best appetizers I've ever had. A friend of mine, Dick Cingolani, who is a chef and restaurant owner in Florida, was kind enough to share it with us. You can buy ready-made taco shells, and most of the other ingredients are available in well-stocked Oriental markets.

**MAKES 6 SERVINGS**

### TACOS
3 tablespoons unsalted butter
24 medium shrimp, shelled and
    deveined
2 tablespoons finely chopped
    garlic
1 cup peeled, seeded, and chopped
    tomato
1½ cups Thai chili sauce for
    chicken
6 prepared corn taco shells
3 cups shredded lettuce
Shredded carrots and black
    sesame seeds for garnish
    (optional)

### COCONUT CURRY SAUCE
2 cans Thai coconut milk,
    unsweetened
1½ tablespoons Thai fish sauce
½ teaspoon turmeric
1 teaspoon Thai curry paste,
    or to taste
Salt and freshly ground white
    pepper to taste

*Make the shrimp:* In a saucepan large enough to hold all the shrimp, heat the butter and when hot, add the shrimp. Cook for 1 minute on each side. Add the garlic and when fragrant (30 seconds maximum), add the tomatoes and chili sauce. Cook for another minute or so, until the shrimp are done.

*Make the sauce:* In a saucepan, gently boil the coconut milk until it is thick enough to coat the back of a spoon. Add the rest of the ingredients, whisk all together, and taste for seasonings.

*To serve:* Place a little shredded lettuce in a taco shell, top with chopped tomato, and lay it on a plate. On top of the taco, place shrimp, spilling out of the shell, drizzle with cooking sauce, and spoon a little coconut sauce next to the shrimp. Garnish with shredded carrots and black sesame seeds, if desired.

# Shrimp Sambuca

*This recipe has been one of the most popular appetizers at The Left Bank (and my cooking classes) for many years. If you are a fan of anisette, or any licorice-flavored liqueur, you'll love it. You can substitute brandy, bourbon, or even tequila for the Sambuca.*

**MAKES 4 SERVINGS**

1½ pounds fresh shrimp
   (16 to 20 per pound),
   peeled and deveined
2 tablespoons unsalted butter,
   divided
1 teaspoon olive oil
2 medium shallots, very finely
   chopped

2 tablespoons dry vermouth
2 tablespoons Sambuca liqueur
½ cup heavy whipping cream
½ cup peeled, seeded, and
   chopped tomatoes
Salt and freshly ground black
   pepper to taste
12 stalks fresh chives, optional

In a skillet large enough to hold the shrimp without crowding, heat 1 tablespoon of the butter and 1 teaspoon olive oil. When light brown in color, add the shrimp and sauté for 2 to 3 minutes. Stir and turn the shrimp, then add the shallots and cook, making sure not to burn them.

Add the vermouth and Sambuca, and let bubble until volume is reduced by half. Add the cream, tomatoes, and salt and pepper. Continue to cook until sauce is thick enough to coat the bottom of a spoon. Remove from heat and stir in the remaining tablespoon of butter (optional, but it helps make a smooth and creamy sauce).

Pour a couple of tablespoons of the finished sauce onto the bottom of a plate, arrange 4 to 5 shrimp in a fan, and decorate with the chives if desired.

# Grilled Scallops

## WITH YELLOW BELL PEPPER–BLACK BEAN SALSA

*Do not overcook the scallops or they'll be dry and tough. Properly grilled scallops should be tender, juicy, and sweet. If Scotch Bonnet chilies aren't available in your area, use any fresh, hot pepper such as jalapeño. Check the grates of your grill before cooking the scallops; if they are too far apart, you may need to skewer the scallops or use a grilling basket to keep them from falling into the fire. I love the flavor combination of yellow peppers and black beans. The yellow pepper gives this tangy salsa a beautiful vivid color. If you don't have any cooked dried black beans on hand, you can use canned black beans, drained and very well rinsed.*

**MAKES 4 SERVINGS**

### SCALLOPS
½ cup olive oil
1 small Scotch Bonnet pepper, chopped and seeded
4 garlic cloves, minced
8 whole black peppercorns
1½ pounds jumbo sea scallops
Salt and freshly ground black pepper to taste

### SALSA
1 large yellow bell pepper, cored, seeded, and roughly chopped
1 tablespoon Dijon mustard
1 tablespoon white wine vinegar
½ cup olive oil
2 tablespoons hot water
¼ teaspoon salt
¼ teaspoon pepper
1 tablespoon fresh cilantro leaves (no stems)
¼ cup cooked black beans

*Marinate the scallops:* Mix the oil, Scotch Bonnet pepper, garlic, and peppercorns in a glass bowl. Add the scallops, mix well, and let rest at room temperature for 1 hour.

*Make the salsa:* Place the chunks of yellow pepper into a blender and add the mustard and vinegar. Blend for 1 minute. Stop and scrape down the sides, if necessary.

Strain the purée through a sieve and return the strained liquid to the blender. Turn on the blender and slowly pour in the olive oil. With the motor still running, add the hot water, salt, and pepper. Add the cilantro and blend 15 more seconds.

Pour the mixture into a serving bowl and stir in the black beans.

The salsa will keep for several days, covered, in the refrigerator. Mix well before using.

*Grill the scallops:* Prepare the grill for high heat. It is important that the grill be very hot, otherwise the scallops will lose their juices. Grill the scallops for 2 minutes on each side, or to your liking. Add salt and pepper.

Serve the scallops immediately with Yellow Bell Pepper–Black Bean Salsa; they should be enjoyed while they are still juicy and steaming.

# Sautéed Scallops Tequila

*In this dish, luscious, velvety-textured scallops bathe in a rich creamy sauce spiked with tequila and orange. You could also grill or broil the scallops and serve them with the sauce. Do not overcook the scallops, whatever method of cooking you choose. A saffron risotto would make a good accompaniment.*

**MAKES 4 SERVINGS**

3 tablespoons unsalted butter, divided
1 tablespoon sunflower oil
1 pound sea scallops (30 to 40 in a pound)
2 shallots, finely chopped
¼ cup rice wine vinegar
¼ cup tequila
¼ cup dry vermouth

2 tablespoons frozen orange juice concentrate, thawed
Finely grated zest of 1 orange (zest is the top layer of the orange peel)
½ cup heavy whipping cream
Freshly ground white pepper and salt to taste

In a large sauté pan, heat 1 tablespoon of the butter and the sunflower oil over medium heat. Add the scallops and sauté for 2 minutes on one side. Turn the scallops, add the shallots, and cook until shallots are translucent, about 2 minutes. Add the vinegar and let bubble until the pan is almost dry.

Add the tequila and vermouth. Let bubble until volume is reduced by half. Stir in the orange concentrate, orange zest, and cream, and lower the heat. Let bubble gently until sauce is thick enough to coat the back of a spoon. Add the remaining butter, 1 tablespoon at a time, and remove immediately from the heat.

Season with white pepper (so there won't be any dark flecks) and salt.

# Crabmeat Crepes

*D*on't be reluctant to make crepes—they're just very thin pancakes and you'll get the hang of them in one or two tries. Strain the batter and let it sit in the refrigerator for a while, so it's silky smooth. This is a show-stopping appetizer for parties, and you can make it ahead of time.

**MAKES 4 SERVINGS**

### CREPES
2 large eggs
1 cup all-purpose flour
1 cup milk
1 tablespoon olive oil
¼ teaspoon puréed fresh garlic
   (peeled and crushed with a
   knife, then very finely chopped
   into a paste)
1 tablespoon unsalted butter
¼ teaspoon salt

### CRABMEAT FILLING
12 ounces cooked crabmeat,
   picked over for shells and
   cartilage
½ cup Aioli plus additional
   for serving (page 240)

¼ cup finely diced, peeled apple
2 dashes hot pepper sauce
Salt and freshly ground black
   pepper to taste
1 whole zucchini, scrubbed well
   under cold water and cut into
   very fine julienne
1 celery stalk, cut into very fine
   julienne
1 large carrot, cut into very fine
   julienne
1 leek, white part only, cut into
   very fine julienne
Salt and freshly ground black
   pepper to taste

*(continued)*

*Make the crepe batter:* Place all ingredients in a bowl or blender, and whisk or blend until very smooth. Strain through a fine sieve into a container, then cover and refrigerate at least 3 hours before using, preferably overnight.

*Make the crepes:* Heat a 6-inch nonstick crepe or omelet pan and grease it with a tiny amount of butter. Pour in about 2 tablespoons of batter and tip the pan to spread the batter evenly and produce a thin, delicate crepe.

Cook the crepe over medium heat until the bottom is lightly browned, then turn it over and brown the other side lightly. Remove to a plate and repeat. Stack the crepes with parchment paper or waxed paper between them to prevent sticking. Wrap the stack and refrigerate until ready to use.

Crepes may be made a day ahead.

*Make the filling:* In a mixing bowl, combine the crabmeat, aioli, apple, hot pepper sauce, and salt and pepper. Mix well.

*Assemble the crepes:* Working with 1 crepe at a time, spoon about ¼ cup of the crabmeat filling into a long, narrow strip across the lower half of the crepe. Arrange a few pieces of each vegetable on top of the crab mixture.

Fold over the flap of the crepe and roll tightly to wrap up the filling. Repeat. The rolled crepes can be refrigerated for a few hours.

To serve, slice each crepe in half at an angle. Stand each cut section of crepe on end, place on the plate, and drizzle with additional Aioli.

# Sliced Duck Breast

## WITH BANANA–CITRUS VINAIGRETTE

*H*ere's an elegant cold appetizer for special occasions. Both the duck and the vinaigrette can be prepared ahead and assembled at the last minute. You may have to ask your butcher to special-order the duck breasts if they're not routinely available at your meat market.

*This vinaigrette adds special flavor to cold, thin-sliced duck breast, and it would also be excellent with grilled chicken breasts or grilled fish. Try it drizzled over a plate of juicy, ripe fruit slices for an unbelievable taste treat.*

**MAKES 4 SERVINGS**

**MARINADE**
½ cup sunflower oil
¼ cup rice wine vinegar
1 tablespoon minced fresh ginger
½ cup pineapple juice
¼ cup dark rum

8 boneless and skinless duck
   breast halves
1 tablespoon unsalted butter
1 tablespoon olive oil
1 cup Banana–Citrus Vinaigrette
   (page 30)

Combine the marinade ingredients in a small bowl. Set the duck breasts in a shallow glass baking dish and pour marinade over them.

Let sit at room temperature for about an hour, then cover and refrigerate for at least 3 hours.

Heat oven to 400°.

Remove the duck breasts from the marinade and discard marinade.

Heat the butter and oil in a large, ovenproof sauté pan over medium-high heat. When very hot, add the duck breasts and let brown for 5 minutes. Turn the duck over, then put the sauté pan in the oven and roast the duck for 7 more minutes. The breasts should be plump and medium rare.

*(continued)*

Remove from the oven and let the duck cool at room temperature for 45 minutes. Set in a container, cover with plastic wrap, and refrigerate for at least 2 to 3 hours. To serve, remove the duck from the refrigerator and thinly slice the breasts lengthwise.

In the center of each plate, place a small ramekin filled with wild rice, brown rice, or couscous. Fan a sliced duck breast half on either side of the ramekin. Ladle 1 tablespoon of vinaigrette on each half and serve.

## BANANA–CITRUS VINAIGRETTE

**MAKES 1½ CUPS**

*1 ripe banana*
*½ cup orange juice*
*1 tablespoon lemon juice*
*1 tablespoon lime juice*
*1 tablespoon apple cider vinegar*
*1 tablespoon Dijon mustard*
*1 peeled tangerine*

*½ teaspoon ground cinnamon*
*½ cup sunflower oil*
*1 teaspoon hot water*
*¼ teaspoon salt*
*¼ teaspoon freshly ground white pepper*

Peel the banana and place all ingredients (except oil, water, salt, and pepper) in a blender. Blend until very smooth, about 1 minute.

Strain the mixture through a fine sieve and reserve only 1 cup. Discard the remainder. Put the cup of purée back in the blender, turn the blender on, and slowly pour in the oil.

When the oil is completely integrated into the mixture, add the hot water, salt and pepper, and blend briefly.

The vinaigrette will keep, covered, in the refrigerator for a few days. Shake it well before using.

# Garlic Crostini

*These delicately perfumed toasts are excellent served with a Caesar or any salad. Make them bite-size and spread them with your favorite topping as an appetizer.*

**MAKES 30 CROSTINI**

1 loaf French or Italian bread, about 18 inches long and 2 inches in diameter
4 tablespoons olive oil for brushing

4 garlic cloves, peeled
1 teaspoon chopped fresh parsley

Preheat grill to high heat.

Cut the bread diagonally into 30 ¼- to ½-inch thick slices. Brush both sides with olive oil. Grill each slice until marked golden brown on each side. If you do not wish to grill the bread, bake it in a preheated 350° oven until each slice is golden brown, about 10 to 15 minutes.

Rub with garlic cloves and sprinkle with chopped parsley.

Serve the crostini with a variety of favorite toppings.

# Mozzarella, Tomato, and Basil Crostini

*This is my quick interpretation of a pizza. These crostini are crunchy and just as tasty. The last drizzle of extra-virgin olive oil gives the crostini a mellow olive flavor that marries beautifully with the mozzarella and tomatoes.*

**MAKES 30 CROSTINI**

1 tablespoon olive oil
3 tablespoons minced red onion
2 tablespoons minced fresh garlic
2 cups peeled, seeded, and
  chopped tomatoes

30 slices of Garlic Crostini
  (page 31)
½ cup chopped fresh mozzarella
2 tablespoons minced fresh sweet
  basil leaves
Extra-virgin olive oil for drizzling

Heat oven to 375°.

In a sauté pan, heat the olive oil and when hot, add the onion. Cook onion until translucent, then add the garlic. When garlic is fragrant, about 1 minute, add the tomatoes. Cook for 3 to 4 minutes.

Top each crostini with about 1 tablespoon of the tomato mixture. Top with the chopped mozzarella. Bake for 5 to 10 minutes. Sprinkle with fresh basil and drizzle ¼ teaspoon of extra-virgin olive oil on each crostini.

# Prosciutto, Leek, and Goat Cheese Crostini

*$\mathcal{M}$ake sure that the prosciutto is paper-thin, so that it will be easy to eat, and just flavor the crostini without overpowering them.*

**MAKES 30 CROSTINI**

1 tablespoon unsalted butter
2 leeks, white part only, well
    washed and cut into very thin
    crosswise slices
5 ounces mild crumbled goat
    cheese

Salt and freshly ground black
    pepper to taste
30 slices Garlic Crostini
    (page 31)
10 paper-thin slices prosciutto, cut
    into thirds crosswise

Heat oven to 350°.

In a sauté pan, heat the butter and cook the leeks on very low heat until soft and translucent, 3 to 5 minutes. Add the goat cheese, salt, and pepper, and cook for 1 minute. Place a thin slice of prosciutto on each crostini and top with the leek mixture. Place on a baking sheet and bake for 3 to 5 minutes.

# Soups

CHILLED BEET AND GINGER SOUP

YELLOW PEPPER AND TOMATO GAZPACHO

STRAWBERRY SOUP

PEAR ALMONDINE SOUP

ROASTED BUTTERNUT SQUASH AND
SHERRY BISQUE

BUTTERNUT SQUASH SOUP

CARROT, GINGER, AND DILL SOUP

SOUPE au PISTOU

SCALLION AND GARLIC SOUP

TOMATO AND PROSCIUTTO SOUP

TOMATO AND TANGERINE SOUP

# Chilled Beet and Ginger Soup

*T*his wonderful soup comes from Hubert Keller, the chef de cuisine of the Fleur de Lys restaurant in San Francisco. This light, fresh, healthy soup has an incredible personality.

**MAKES 4 SERVINGS**

8 medium-size beets, peeled
½ ounce peeled ginger
2 peeled garlic cloves
3 tablespoons homemade
    mayonnaise (page 239)
1 lemon, juiced

1 teaspoon rice wine vinegar
Salt and freshly ground white
    pepper to taste
½ cup baby peas, blanched
4 pinches dried chervil

Cut the peeled beets into small pieces. Run the peeled ginger, beets, and garlic cloves through a juicer. Transfer the juice into a mixing bowl. Add the mayonnaise, lemon juice, vinegar, salt, and pepper. Mix well and refrigerate.

Just before serving, check the seasoning and add the blanched baby peas. Ladle the soup into shallow-rimmed soup plates and sprinkle with chervil.

Serve a baguette of freshly baked French bread on the side.

# Yellow Pepper and Tomato Gazpacho

*T*his recipe makes enough soup for one 8-ounce bowl per person, so you'll have to blend the soup in batches, then stir them together. To increase the yield, make sure to adjust each measurement. This soup is not only addictive (you may not be able to stop eating it), it also has eye appeal because you use only yellow peppers and yellow tomatoes. If yellow tomatoes are unavailable, substitute juicy red, vine-ripened ones. Red bell peppers will create a gorgeous red soup. Yellow bell peppers and red tomatoes make the soup turn a mellow, yellow-orange.

**MAKES 8 SERVINGS**

4 large yellow tomatoes, peeled, seeded, and cut into chunks
2 yellow bell peppers, seeded and cut into chunks
2 peeled European cucumbers, peeled, halved lengthwise, and seeds removed (see Note)
3 garlic cloves, minced
½ white onion, chopped
1 tablespoon rice wine vinegar
1 tablespoon lemon juice
¼ cup olive oil

½ cup Chicken Stock (page 233)
1 small yellow Scotch Bonnet, or yellow Tabasco, or yellow habanero pepper (remove the seeds and ribs for less heat)
1 tablespoon white wine Worcestershire sauce
Salt and freshly ground white pepper to taste
1 tablespoon fresh cilantro leaves
1 cup Chive Crème Fraîche (page 241)

For garnish reserve ¼ cup each of the tomatoes, peppers, and cucumbers, cut into ¼-inch squares.

Working in batches, in the blender combine the remaining tomatoes, bell peppers, and cucumbers, and the garlic, onion, vinegar, lemon juice, olive oil, chicken stock, chili pepper, and Worcestershire sauce. Blend until very smooth. Season with salt and pepper, add the cilantro, and blend for

15 to 20 more seconds. Remove from the blender, add the reserved vegetables, and chill thoroughly.

After the soup is chilled, you can adjust the seasonings by adding a bit more lemon juice, salt or pepper, or perhaps a touch of Tabasco. It should taste slightly spicy.

Top each serving with Chive Crème Fraîche. Serve ice cold.

**NOTE:** European, or English, cucumbers are meatier and have fewer seeds. You need to peel them, as you do not want the bright green skin to darken this golden soup.

# Strawberry Soup

*I* love to serve an ice-cold fruit soup for an early-summer dinner party. This is a very simple, low-fat recipe and can be prepared the day before.

**MAKES 4 SERVINGS**

2 cups strawberries, washed and
   stems removed (reserve 4
   for garnish)
½ cup orange juice
1 tablespoon vodka

1 cup low-fat vanilla yogurt
1 tablespoon lemon juice
Salt and freshly ground black
   pepper to taste
Mint leaves, for garnish

In a food processor or blender, combine all ingredients except mint. Blend until very smooth. Strain through a fine sieve. Chill until very cold.

Serve in very cold soup plates. Garnish with a strawberry and fresh mint leaves on each plate.

# Pear Almondine Soup

*This glorious soup is so fruity and smooth that you might want it for dessert! But it really works best as the first course for a casual or elegant dinner. Or serve it in a mug for lunch on a steamy summer day.*

**MAKES 4 SERVINGS**

*4 fresh pears (they do not have
  to be ripe)*
*2 cups water*
*1 tablespoon vanilla extract*
*¼ cup blanched almonds*

*¼ cup Amaretto liqueur*
*1¾ cups (14 ounces) plain yogurt*
*Salt and freshly ground white
  pepper to taste*

Peel, core, and chop the pears. Place them in a large saucepan with the water and vanilla, and bring to a boil. Lower heat and simmer until tender.

Combine the cooked pears, almonds, and Amaretto in a blender, and purée until very smooth. Add the yogurt and blend 30 more seconds. You may need to do this in batches. Add salt and pepper and chill, covered, until very cold, at least 8 hours.

# Roasted Butternut Squash and Sherry Bisque

*R*oasting a beautiful butternut squash intensifies its flavor and sweetness, making it a wonderful foundation for a creamy, elegant soup. The sherry adds a subtle, special touch.

**MAKES 4 TO 6 SERVINGS**

2 medium butternut squash,
   about 3 pounds total
2 tablespoons sunflower oil
   (see Note)
2 medium onions, chopped, about
   1½ cups
1 tablespoon finely chopped fresh
   ginger
½ cup dry sherry (see Note)
¼ cup bourbon, optional
5 cups Chicken Stock (page 233)

2 tablespoons arrowroot
   (see Note)
3 tablespoons cold water
1 cup heavy whipping cream
4 tablespoons (½ stick) unsalted
   butter, optional
Salt and freshly ground white
   pepper to taste
6 sprigs fresh cilantro, finely
   chopped, optional

With a sharp knife, prick the squash in several places to allow air to escape while it cooks (otherwise, it could burst). Heat the oven to 375°, place the squash in a baking dish lined with foil, and roast for about 90 minutes, or until the squash is soft when pressed. Let cool for 30 minutes, then peel, seed, and remove the strings. Cut the roasted squash into ½-inch pieces.

In a heavy soup kettle, heat the oil, then add the onions and cook over medium heat until they are translucent but not browned, about 10 minutes. Add the ginger and stir for 2 minutes. Add the sherry and bourbon, if using, and let bubble briskly until the volume is reduced by half. Now add the squash and stock, bring the pot to a boil, then lower the heat, and cook gently until the squash is completely tender, 5 to 10 minutes.

Purée the soup in a blender, food processor, food mill or, better yet, a hand-held immersion blender (page 11). Return the puréed soup to the kettle; dissolve the arrowroot in the water and stir the mixture into the soup. It will thicken immediately. Add the cream, then stir in the optional butter, a pat at a time, to give the soup a creamy, rich taste.

Season with salt and pepper, then serve with cilantro sprinkled on top, if desired.

**NOTE:** I like the buttery taste of sunflower oil. And I prefer to thicken soups with arrowroot because it doesn't have the floury taste that cornstarch has. Arrowroot is a white powder that can be found in the spice section of your supermarket.

Do not use heavily salted cooking sherry in this or any other recipe. Instead, use a good-quality dry cocktail sherry.

# Butternut Squash Soup

*I* love the yellow color and sweet, buttery taste of butternut squash, so here's a chunky, country-style soup based on it. Top each serving with a sprig of thyme. My sous-chef, Bradley, created this delicious soup for Sunshine Cuisine.

**MAKES 2¼ QUARTS, OR TEN 8-OUNCE SERVINGS**

1 tablespoon olive oil
2 cups chopped white onion, cut into ½-inch pieces
1 cup chopped celery, about 3 stalks, cut into ½-inch pieces
1 cup chopped red bell pepper (1 medium pepper, cut into ½-inch pieces)
2 teaspoons chopped fresh thyme leaves

4 cups peeled butternut squash (see Note), cut into ½-inch cubes
2 teaspoons minced fresh garlic
6 cups Vegetable Stock (page 231) or Chicken Stock (page 233)
Salt and pepper to taste

Heat the olive oil in a large saucepan over medium heat and sauté the onion until translucent.

Add the celery and red bell pepper, and sauté for a few minutes. Add the thyme and squash cubes, and sauté for 5 minutes.

Add the garlic and, when fragrant, add the stock and bring to a simmer. Cook until the squash is completely tender, about 20 minutes. Add salt and pepper.

**NOTE:** The best way to peel a hard squash such as butternut is to cut it into manageable chunks or slices, then stand them on a cutting board and use a sharp knife to trim off the peel as you would a melon. The skin is too tough to tackle with a vegetable peeler.

# Carrot, Ginger, and Dill Soup

*In this great and easy-to-make soup, ginger jazzes up sweet orange carrots, topped off with fresh green dill.*

**MAKES 4 SERVINGS**

| | |
|---|---|
| 1 tablespoon unsalted butter | 4 cups peeled and chopped carrots |
| 1 tablespoon olive oil | 6 cups Chicken Stock (page 233) |
| 1 cup minced onion | Salt and freshly ground black |
| 2 tablespoons minced fresh ginger | pepper to taste |
| 1 tablespoon minced fresh garlic | 2 tablespoons chopped fresh dill |

In a soup kettle, heat the butter and olive oil. When the butter and oil start to foam, add the onion and cook until translucent but not browned. Add the ginger and garlic. Sauté for 1 minute, add the carrots and stock.

Reduce heat to low, cover, and let simmer for 1 hour and 10 minutes, until carrots are tender. Purée the soup until very smooth in a blender, food processor, food mill, or hand-held immersion blender (page 11).

Strain the soup through a fine sieve into a large bowl. With a wooden spoon or spatula, press or purée the vegetables to extract all their juices.

Season with salt and pepper and freshly chopped dill.

# Soupe au Pistou

*This* *is one of my favorite soups. When my mother used to make Soupe au Pistou, the entire house smelled of basil and garlic. She cooked it in a huge soup kettle and we would eat it for lunch and dinner, two days in a row. The soup is so filling, don't plan on preparing any main course. A small green salad will do just fine.*

**MAKES 8 SERVINGS**

*1 tablespoon olive oil*
*1 cup onion, peeled and cut into ¼-inch cubes*
*1 cup carrots, peeled and cut into ¼-inch cubes*
*1 cup white potatoes, peeled and cut into ¼-inch cubes*
*1 pound green beans, ends removed, cut into 1-inch pieces*
*2 tablespoons minced garlic*
*3 cups peeled, seeded, and chopped tomatoes*
*2 cups Chicken Stock (page 233)*
*2 cups Brown Beef Stock (page 236)*

*2 large zucchini, well scrubbed and cut into ¼-inch cubes*
*2 yellow squash, well scrubbed and cut into ¼-inch cubes*
*1 cup eggplant, cut into ¼-inch cubes*
*1 cup cooked white beans*
*1 cup cooked red kidney beans*
*1 cup cooked pinto beans*
*¼ cup packed fresh sweet basil leaves*
*Salt and freshly ground black pepper to taste*
*1 cup Almond Pesto (page 242)*

In a large soup kettle, heat the olive oil. When oil is hot, add the onion. When onion is translucent, add the carrots, potatoes, and green beans. Sauté for 5 minutes, or until the potatoes start to color slightly. Add the garlic and when fragrant, add the tomatoes and chicken and beef stocks.

Cover, reduce heat, and cook for 15 minutes. Add the zucchini, yellow squash, and eggplant. Cover again and cook for 15 more minutes. Add all the cooked beans, the basil, salt, and pepper, and cook for 5 more minutes.

Place 1 tablespoon of pesto in the middle of each soup plate, pour the soup over it, and serve.

# Scallion and Garlic Soup

*Who do you think gave me this recipe? You guessed it, my mother. It is thick, silky like pale velvet, and absolutely irresistible. And it's also easy to make. Season the soup with white pepper so there won't be any black specks in it.*

**MAKES 4 SERVINGS**

2 large heads garlic
1 tablespoon unsalted butter
1 tablespoon olive oil
1 large onion, peeled and chopped
3 scallions, chopped
2 cups Chicken Stock (page 233)
4 medium red potatoes, peeled
   and cut into chunks

1 cup heavy whipping cream
1 cup milk
Salt and freshly ground white
   pepper to taste
1 tablespoon chopped fresh
   cilantro leaves

Separate the cloves of the heads of garlic, but do not peel them. Bring two small saucepans of water to boil, then put the garlic in one of them. Poach for 5 minutes, then drain and return the garlic to the other pot of boiling water. Let cook 5 minutes, then drain and return garlic to the first pot, once again filled with boiling water, for final blanching. This will eliminate any bitterness.

Cool the garlic briefly, then slip the cloves out of their skins.

In a soup kettle, heat the butter and olive oil. Add the onion and scallions, and sauté for 3 to 4 minutes.

Add the poached garlic, stock, and potatoes. Cook for 35 minutes until potatoes are very soft. Insert a hand-held immersion (page 11) blender into the soup kettle and purée, or transfer soup into a blender in batches and blend very well.

Return the purée to the soup pot, then stir in the cream and milk. Bring to a boil, reduce heat, and cook for 10 more minutes. Adjust salt and pepper and add the chopped cilantro.

# Tomato and Proscuitto Soup

*To make this intensely flavored, smooth soup into a fantastic chunky, country-style soup, just chop the celery a little more finely, and peel, seed, and chop the tomatoes before adding them. Don't purée the chunky version. The more refined, puréed version is an excellent starter before a casual dinner.*

**MAKES 4 SERVINGS**

*1 tablespoon olive oil*
*1 large onion, finely chopped*
*2 celery stalks, cut into ½-inch pieces*
*1 medium green bell pepper, seeded and finely chopped*
*1 medium red bell pepper, seeded and finely chopped*
*1 tablespoon finely chopped garlic (about 4 cloves)*
*3 pounds large, ripe tomatoes (about 5), cored and chopped*

*4 cups Chicken Stock (page 233)*
*2 sprigs fresh thyme or 1 teaspoon dried thyme*
*2 sprigs fresh oregano or 1 teaspoon dried oregano*
*3 sprigs fresh cilantro*
*1 tablespoon olive oil*
*4 ounces prosciutto, pancetta, or lean bacon, cut into ¼-inch strips*
*Salt and freshly ground pepper to taste*

Heat olive oil in a large, nonaluminum soup kettle (see Note) over medium heat, then add onion and cook, stirring occasionally, for about 10 minutes, until onion is translucent and soft. Do not let onion brown. Add the celery and bell peppers, and cook, stirring, for 5 minutes. Now, add the garlic and stir for a minute (*do not* let the garlic brown or burn). The moment you smell the aroma of the garlic, add the tomatoes and stock. Stir in the herbs, then bring the mixture to a boil. Reduce the heat to low and let simmer for 30 minutes.

Purée the soup until very smooth in a blender, food processor, food mill, or hand-held immersion blender (page 11). Strain the soup through a fine sieve into a large bowl. Use a wooden spoon or spatula to press on the puréed vegetables to extract all their juices.

Rinse the soup kettle and return it to the stove on medium heat. Add the remaining tablespoon of olive oil and heat, then add the prosciutto and sauté for 1 to 2 minutes. Return the puréed soup to the pot carefully—watch out for splattering—and let it simmer over low heat for about 30 minutes.

Season to taste with salt and freshly ground black pepper. To serve, float a spoonful of Almond Pesto (page 242) in each bowl, if desired.

**NOTE:** Never cook acidic foods like tomatoes or make recipes that contain wine, vinegar, or lemon juice in an aluminum pot because the food will react with the metal and pick up a "tinny" taste. Instead, choose stainless steel, enameled cast-iron, or nonstick cookware.

# Tomato and Tangerine Soup

*I* love to serve this soup for an elegant dinner party. Strikingly orange in color, beautifully fragrant, and absolutely delicious hot or cold. For a simpler version, just use the tangerine juice, stock, and tomatoes. A dollop of crème fraîche or sour cream is a rich finishing touch.

**MAKES 4 SERVINGS**

4–6 tangerines, to yield
   2 teaspoons grated zest
   and 1 cup juice
1 tablespoon sunflower oil
½ cup chopped white onion
1 teaspoon curry powder
1 medium leek, white part only,
   chopped

6 cups peeled, seeded, and
   chopped tomatoes (about
   6 tomatoes)
2 cups Chicken Stock (page 233)
Salt and freshly ground black
   pepper to taste

Wash the tangerines and grate enough zest (the orange-colored top layer of the peel) to equal 2 teaspoons.

Juice the tangerines, removing any seeds, to make 1 cup.

Heat the oil in a 6-quart pot over medium heat. Add the onion and cook until translucent, about 5 minutes. Add the curry powder and leek, and sauté for a couple of minutes. Add the tomatoes, grated zest, and stock. Cook on medium heat, stirring occasionally, for 15 minutes.

Stir in the tangerine juice, salt, and pepper. Purée very finely in a blender or with a hand-held immersion blender (page 11).

Serve hot immediately or chill, covered, in the refrigerator for 8 to 10 hours.

# Salads

GRILLED EGGPLANT AND ROASTED RED PEPPERS

LEFT BANK CAESAR SALAD WITH FONTINA CROUTONS

LEEK SALAD WITH ROASTED SHALLOT VINAIGRETTE

CURRIED ENDIVE SALAD

NEW POTATOES AND BEET SALAD WITH
SCALLION VINAIGRETTE

MUSHROOM AND VIDALIA ONION SALAD

RADISH AND CUCUMBER SALAD WITH
CHIVE VINAIGRETTE

VINE-RIPENED TOMATO SALAD WITH SWEET BASIL
VINAIGRETTE

SHRIMP SALAD AIOLI

LIME SCALLOP SALAD

SESAME-CRUSTED TUNA ON MIXED GREENS

CHICKEN SALAD WITH RED PEPPER AND
GRILLED CORN VINAIGRETTE

GRILLED CHICKEN SALAD WITH CHILI MAYONNAISE

PORK TENDERLOIN AND COUSCOUS SALAD

# Grilled Eggplant and Roasted Red Peppers

*G*rilling lends a smoky, delicious taste to eggplant and makes it a summer-perfect salad. Roasted red bell peppers add color and a rich sweetness. I like to roast bell peppers in advance and keep them in olive oil in the refrigerator. The Balsamic Vinaigrette is a simple, basic dressing that can be used with different salads.

**MAKES 4 SERVINGS**

### SALAD
3 large red bell peppers
2 small eggplants
⅓ cup olive oil, combined with
    3 cloves minced garlic

### BALSAMIC VINAIGRETTE
1 tablespoon Dijon mustard
1 tablespoon balsamic vinegar
½ cup olive oil
Salt and freshly ground black
    pepper to taste

*Make the salad:* Place the bell peppers on an open gas burner until the skin blisters and turns completely black. You can achieve the same result on a grill or under the broiler in your oven. Transfer peppers to a plastic bag and close securely to let them steam for 20 minutes.

Scrape off the charred skin, then remove the stems and seeds. Try to remove all without rinsing the peppers under water, as you would lose too much of the roasted flavor. Cut the roasted peppers into thin julienne strips and set aside.

Cut the eggplant lengthwise into ¼-inch slices. Brush the slices with the garlic oil and let rest for 15 minutes to absorb its flavor. Grill over a very hot grill until browned on each side, about 5 to 7 minutes.

*Make the vinaigrette:* In a glass bowl, combine all ingredients and mix well.

*To serve:* Arrange the eggplant slices on a serving platter and drizzle with the vinaigrette. Top with the roasted bell peppers.

# Left Bank Caesar Salad

## WITH FONTINA CROUTONS

*I receive many requests for this salad from loyal customers at The Left Bank. What makes it so special is that all the ingredients are emulsified together so that they become one single ingredient . . . with the fragrance of garlic and a slight background flavor of anchovies. At The Left Bank we prepare this salad in a large wooden bowl that has been carefully seasoned with garlic and black pepper. This quick version will produce almost the same result. Homemade croutons may seem like a bit of work, but I promise you that once you've tasted their great flavor and texture, you will never buy another box from the store! So give it a go! You won't be sorry.*

**MAKES 4 SERVINGS**

### FONTINA CROUTONS
*10 slices day-old French bread, approximately ½ inch thick and 2½ inches round*
*3 large garlic cloves, for rubbing the bread*
*2 tablespoons unsalted butter*
*2 tablespoons olive oil*
*2 tablespoons minced garlic*
*½ cup freshly grated Fontina or Parmigiano-Reggiano cheese*

### CAESAR SALAD
*4 heads romaine lettuce, center leaves only*
*2 egg yolks*
*1 tablespoon Dijon mustard*
*2 large anchovies*
*1 tablespoon minced garlic*
*1 teaspoon Worcestershire sauce*
*1 tablespoon red wine vinegar*
*½ cup sunflower oil*
*1 tablespoon fresh lemon juice*
*¼ teaspoon salt*
*¼ teaspoon freshly grated black pepper*
*½ cup freshly grated Parmigiano-Reggiano cheese*

*Make the croutons:* If your bread is fresh and you cannot wait for the bread to dry, follow these directions.

Heat oven to 400°. Cut crusts off the bread and place slices, in a single layer, on a baking sheet. Place in the oven, *turn oven off,* and leave inside for 30 to 45 minutes until dry. Peel the garlic and rub it on both sides of the dried bread. Cut the bread into ½-inch cubes.

Heat the oven to 300°.

In a large sauté pan, heat the butter and olive oil. When hot, add the garlic and croutons. When the croutons are well coated, remove from heat and add the grated Fontina. Mix well to coat the croutons. This process should take only a minute or two.

Transfer to a baking sheet in a single layer and bake for 15 minutes, or until croutons are golden brown and crisp on all sides.

Allow to cool.

*Make the salad:* You will need about 1 head of romaine lettuce per person, since only the tender, crisp inner leaves are used. Wash the romaine and dry thoroughly with a salad spinner (or with paper towels). The leaves should be extremely dry.

In a food processor, combine the egg yolks, mustard, anchovies, garlic, Worcestershire sauce, and vinegar. Blend until smooth. With the machine running, add the oil slowly. Add the lemon juice, salt, and pepper.

Transfer the dressing to a large salad bowl, cover with the romaine leaves, and toss well until the leaves glisten. Add the croutons and mix well. Add the cheese and mix well.

**NOTE:** The order in which you add the ingredients is very important. First, the salad leaves should be well coated with dressing, so then the croutons will absorb any extra dressing. And lastly the cheese should not be soaked with the dressing, as that would interfere with its flavor and texture.

# Leek Salad

## WITH ROASTED SHALLOT VINAIGRETTE

*W*hen I was growing up, leek salads were often served at our table. I love
their soft texture and sweet onion flavor, and cooking them gently in sugared
water emphasizes the sweetness. The dressing is a rich and creamy
vinaigrette flavored with roasted shallots.

**MAKES 4 SERVINGS**

**SALAD**
4 large leeks, 1 to 1¼ inch thick
¼ cup sugar
8 cups cold water

**ROASTED SHALLOT
VINAIGRETTE**
1 tablespoon olive oil
10 large shallots, peeled and
    cut in half

1 tablespoon fresh rosemary leaves
1 tablespoon Dijon mustard
1 large egg
1 tablespoon white wine vinegar
½ cup olive oil
Salt and freshly ground black
    pepper to taste
2 tablespoons hot water

*Make the salad:* Trim the tough green tops from the leeks, then slit
them lengthwise into quarters. Do not cut through the root end. Rinse the
leeks thoroughly under cold running water, fanning the leaves with your
fingers to release any sand.

Place the leeks in a large saucepan. Mix the sugar and water until the
sugar dissolves, then pour over the leeks. Bring to a boil, then reduce heat
and cook slowly for 20 to 25 minutes, or until tender.

Drain the hot water in the pan and replace it with cold water. Cool the
leeks, drain, and place in a covered container. Refrigerate until very cold.

*Make the vinaigrette:* Heat oven to 400°. In a small baking pan, combine
1 tablespoon olive oil, 7 of the shallots, and the rosemary. Cover with aluminum foil and roast for 20 minutes. Remove from the oven. Place roasted
shallots in a blender and add the mustard, egg, vinegar, ½ cup oil, salt, and
pepper. Blend well. Add the hot water and blend for 15 more seconds. Strain

through a fine sieve. Add the remaining 3 shallots, sliced very thin cross-wise, to the vinaigrette.

Arrange the leeks on a serving platter or individual salad plates and drizzle with the vinaigrette.

# Curried Endive Salad

*Endive, a pale, torpedo-shaped lettuce, has a slightly bittersweet flavor that teams well with oranges, raisins, and curry. This cool, exotic salad takes only minutes to make.*

**MAKES 4 SERVINGS**

*3 large Belgian endive*
*2 large oranges*
*1 egg yolk*
*1 teaspoon curry powder*
*¼ teaspoon cayenne pepper*
*1 tablespoon white wine vinegar*

*½ cup olive oil*
*½ cup plain yogurt*
*Salt and freshly ground black*
  *pepper to taste*
*2 tablespoons raisins*
*2 tablespoons Grand Marnier,*
  *optional*

Clean and chop the endive into 1-inch pieces and set aside.

Peel the skin and white pith from the oranges with a sharp knife. Cut between the dividing membranes to release the orange sections. Set the orange wedges aside.

In a blender, combine the egg yolk, curry powder, cayenne pepper, vinegar, and olive oil, and blend well. Add the yogurt, salt, and pepper, and blend briefly.

In a glass bowl, combine the raisins and Grand Marnier, if using; let rest for 2 minutes. Add the endive and about half the dressing. Toss well; add more dressing if needed.

Divide the endive salad among 4 plates and decorate with the orange segments.

# New Potatoes and Beet Salad

## WITH SCALLION VINAIGRETTE

*Beautiful red beets, with their robust flavor and intense color, are an underappreciated vegetable. In this simple salad, the scallion vinaigrette brings out their special flavor. This salad can also be dressed with a mild vinaigrette of white wine vinegar and flavorful walnut oil, tossed with toasted walnut halves. The creamy vinaigrette has a very distinct scallion-and-onion flavor and the Calamata olives (which you should not add until the last minute) give it a wonderful Mediterranean touch. This vinaigrette goes well with potato salad, pork tenderloin, or lamb chops.*

**MAKES 4 SERVINGS**

**SALAD**

1 pound fresh red beets
2 pounds red potatoes
1 teaspoon salt
2 scallions, cut diagonally,
 $\frac{1}{16}$ inch thick
Salt and freshly ground black
 pepper to taste

**SCALLION VINAIGRETTE**

3 scallions, chopped fine
1 medium onion, peeled and
 chopped fine
3 garlic cloves, peeled
1 tablespoon white wine vinegar
2 tablespoons hot water
1 tablespoon Dijon mustard
1 egg yolk
½ cup olive oil
1 dozen Calamata olives, pitted
 and chopped
1 tablespoon chopped fresh parsley

*Make the salad:* Trim the leaves from the beets, leaving 1 inch of stem (to keep them from "bleeding" into the cooking water). Rinse the beets well and place in a saucepan. Cover with cold water and bring to a boil. Reduce heat and cook for 30 to 40 minutes, or until tender.

Drain the hot water and replace with cold water. Peel the beets with a small, sharp knife and trim the remaining stems while the beets are still hot. Dice beets into ¼-inch pieces and set aside.

Place the potatoes in a saucepan, cover with cold water, add the salt, and bring to a boil. Reduce heat and cook for 25 to 30 minutes, or until tender. Do not overcook, as the potatoes should still be slightly firm. Drain the hot water and replace with cold water. Peel the potatoes and cut into ¼-inch pieces.

*Make the dressing:* In a blender or food processor, combine the scallions, onion, garlic, vinegar, and water. Blend until very liquid, about 3 to 4 minutes. Strain through a fine sieve by pushing the juice through the mesh.

There should be about ½ cup of thick liquid. Discard any extra liquid. Return mixture to the blender and, with the motor running, add the mustard and egg yolk. Drizzle in the olive oil and blend for 2 minutes. Empty the blender into a bowl and stir in the olives and parsley.

*To serve:* In a large salad bowl, combine the potatoes, beets, scallions, salt, and pepper, and drizzle with Scallion Vinaigrette. Toss gently and serve at room temperature. To serve salad cold, refrigerate all the ingredients separately and assemble them at the last minute.

# Mushroom and Vidalia Onion Salad

*The softness and sweetness of a good Vidalia onion are very appealing. To make this dish even more special (and a bit more costly), use a mix of very fresh wild mushrooms. (When Felicia tested this recipe, she liked it so much that she ate it all herself!)*

**MAKES 4 SERVINGS**

**SALAD**

16 ounces white button
   mushrooms
1 tablespoon olive oil
1 small, sweet Vidalia onion,
   thinly sliced
1 tablespoon fresh thyme leaves,
   chopped
1 tablespoon minced garlic

2 tablespoons Chardonnay or
   other dry white wine
1 tablespoon white wine vinegar

**DRESSING**

1 tablespoon Dijon mustard
1 tablespoon white wine vinegar
½ cup olive oil
Salt and freshly ground black
   pepper to taste

*Make the salad:* Cut the mushrooms in quarters. In a large sauté pan, heat the olive oil. When the oil is hot, add the mushrooms and sauté briefly. Add the onion and thyme. Add the garlic and when the aroma becomes fragrant, add the wine and vinegar. Cook until liquid has evaporated. Remove from the heat, transfer to a bowl, and refrigerate for 2 hours.

*Make the vinaigrette:* In a small bowl, beat together the mustard and vinegar with a fork. While beating (as if you were scrambling eggs), add the olive oil a little at a time. The mixture will be thick and glossy. Add the salt and pepper. (You will use only about half this much dressing on the mushrooms. The rest will keep in the refrigerator for a day or so and is good tossed in a green salad.)

Mix the vinaigrette with the mushrooms. Toss well and serve.

# Radish and Cucumber Salad

## WITH CHIVE VINAIGRETTE

*Peppery scarlet radishes make this a colorful and refreshing summer salad. Use a mandoline, if you have one, to slice the vegetables, but be careful. The blade is sharp. Otherwise, slice as thinly as possible using a knife.*

**MAKES 4 SERVINGS**

### CHIVE VINAIGRETTE
1 tablespoon white wine vinegar
½ cup olive oil
4 chives, finely chopped
Salt and freshly ground black
    pepper to taste

### SALAD
24 large red radishes, cleaned
    and sliced ¹⁄₁₆ inch thick
1 large European cucumber,
    sliced ¹⁄₁₆ inch thick

In a bowl, mix the vinegar, olive oil, chives, salt, and pepper. Add the radishes and cucumbers, and toss to coat. Let stand at room temperature for an hour or serve immediately.

# Vine-Ripened Tomato Salad

## WITH SWEET BASIL VINAIGRETTE

*I was literally raised on this salad. My grandmother and my mother, and now all five of her children are hooked on it. Its success depends upon vine-ripened tomatoes and fresh sweet basil. Serve as an appetizer, between courses, or even as a side dish. Just make sure that the tomatoes and the vinaigrette have time to interact. The tomatoes should release their juices, which will then sweeten the vinaigrette and give it a fruity flavor.*

**MAKES 4 SERVINGS**

4 large, vine-ripened tomatoes
Salt and freshly ground black
    pepper to taste

**SWEET BASIL VINAIGRETTE**
2 tablespoons Dijon mustard
1 egg yolk
1 tablespoon balsamic vinegar

1 tablespoon minced garlic
½ cup extra-virgin olive oil
Salt and freshly ground black
    pepper to taste
1 tablespoon hot water
¼ cup packed sweet basil leaves
    (no stems)

*Make the salad:* Core and slice the tomatoes approximately ¼ inch thick. Arrange in a shallow glass container or a deep plate. Sprinkle with salt and pepper.

*Make the vinaigrette:* In a blender, combine the mustard, egg yolk, vinegar, and garlic. Blend and add the oil, salt and pepper, and 1 tablespoon hot water. Blend a few seconds until smooth. Add the basil leaves and blend for a few more seconds.

*To serve:* Drizzle vinaigrette on tomatoes; let stand up to an hour.

# Shrimp Salad Aioli

*I love the flavor of garlic with shrimp, apples, and celery. The combination of textures and tastes is sensational. Serve this salad with mixed greens inside an avocado half.*

**MAKES 4 SERVINGS**

1 bay leaf
12 whole black peppercorns
2 celery stalks, chopped into 4
    pieces
1 pound small shrimp (61 to 70
    per pound), peeled and
    deveined
¾ cup Aioli (page 240)

2 red apples, cored and diced into
    ¼-inch pieces
2 tablespoons chopped walnuts
2 celery stalks, cut into ¼-inch
    pieces
Salt and freshly ground black
    pepper to taste

Fill a saucepan with water, add the bay leaf, peppercorns, and chopped celery stalks, and bring to a boil. Add the shrimp and cook for 3 to 4 minutes, just until shrimp are opaque, not translucent. Drain and let cool.

In a large glass or ceramic bowl, combine the Aioli (page 240), cooled shrimp, apples, walnuts, and celery pieces. Mix carefully. Add salt and pepper, taste, and adjust seasoning.

# Lime Scallop Salad

*T*he citric acid in the lime juice "cooks" the scallops in this variation on the classic seafood salad called seviche. Be sure the tiny bay scallops are very fresh. For a stunning presentation cut the cucumber slices very thin.

**MAKES 4 SERVINGS**

1 pound bay scallops

**MARINADE**
1 cup lime juice, about 8 juicy limes
¼ cup finely minced onion
1 small pimiento or other hot red pepper, finely minced
1 tablespoon minced fresh ginger

1 tablespoon minced garlic
2 tablespoons minced fresh dill

2 large European cucumbers
1 tablespoon Dijon mustard
1 tablespoon rice wine vinegar
½ cup olive oil
Salt and freshly ground black pepper to taste

*To marinate the scallops:* Place the scallops in a glass or stainless steel container. Combine the marinade ingredients and pour over the scallops. Make sure the scallops are completely covered in marinade, cover the container, and refrigerate overnight.

*To serve:* Cut 1 cucumber into quarters lengthwise and scrape off the seeds. Slice very thinly, making small triangles.

Slice the other cucumber into ¹⁄₁₆-inch (or thinner) round slices. Arrange the slices neatly in a spiral on 4 chilled salad plates. Start on the outside of the plate and work toward the center, overlapping the slices so that they cover the bottom of each plate. Use more cucumber, if necessary.

In a glass bowl, mix together the mustard, vinegar, oil, salt, and pepper. Drain the scallops well, then add to the dressing with the cucumber triangles. Gently spoon the salad onto the center of each prepared plate.

# Sesame-Crusted Tuna on Mixed Greens

*This is a beautiful and exotic salad. Make sure that all the ingredients are very cold and that the mixed greens (called "mesclun") are dry and crisp! Wasabi is a pale green powdered horseradish used in Japanese cooking. Wasabi is very pungent, so use it sparingly!*

**MAKES 4 SERVINGS**

### MESCLUN SALAD
1 cup chopped red leaf lettuce
1 cup chopped green leaf lettuce
1 cup chopped chicory
1 cup chopped arugula
1 cup chopped endive

### WASABI AND SOY VINAIGRETTE
1 teaspoon wasabi
2 tablespoons soy sauce
2 garlic cloves, peeled
1 tablespoon minced fresh ginger
Juice of 1 lemon
1 tablespoon balsamic vinegar

¾ tablespoon olive oil
2 tablespoons hot water
Salt and freshly ground black pepper to taste

### TUNA
2 pieces of fresh tuna, about 1½ inches round or square and 4 inches long
¼ cup olive oil
A mixture of 2 tablespoons white sesame seeds, 2 tablespoons black sesame seeds, and 1 tablespoon freshly ground black pepper

*Make the salad:* Dissolve the wasabi in the soy sauce. In a blender, combine the garlic, ginger, lemon juice, vinegar, and the soy sauce–wasabi mixture. Mix well. Add the olive oil, hot water, and blend. Season with salt and pepper, and pour into a large glass bowl. Add all the greens and mix well. Arrange the greens on salad plates and refrigerate while you prepare the tuna.

*Make the tuna:* Brush the tuna with olive oil, making sure all sides are lightly and evenly coated. Dip each fillet in the sesame-seed mixture, making sure that no tuna is visible, only the sesame seeds. Heat a nonstick frying pan and sear the tuna on all sides for a couple of minutes. Remove from the heat. The tuna should remain rare. Slice tuna very thin, about ⅛ inch, and arrange all the way around the mesclun salad.

# Chicken Salad

## WITH RED PEPPER AND GRILLED CORN VINAIGRETTE

*At the Left Bank we used to prepare this fantastic salad for lunch. The key to its great success is to make sure that the salad is very cold and crisp (mix in the dressing at the last minute), and that the chicken is right off the grill and cut very thin. Great for a weekend lunch or a light dinner. Just get the greens ready, make the vinaigrette, then grill the chicken. Besides accompanying grilled chicken, this pretty vinaigrette would also be great with a moist and tender swordfish or meaty grilled yellowfin tuna steak. The corn adds a nice crunchy texture and grilled flavor.*

**MAKES 4 SERVINGS**

### SALAD

2 cups romaine leaves, cut into
  bite-size pieces
1 cup red leaf lettuce, cut into
  bite-size pieces
1 cup watercress leaves, cut into
  bite-size pieces
1 small red onion, cut into very
  thin slices and separated into
  rings
4 chicken breast halves (about
  6 ounces each), skinned
  and boned

### RED PEPPER AND GRILLED CORN VINAIGRETTE

2 large red bell peppers, cored,
  seeded, and chopped
1 small pimiento
1 tablespoon Dijon mustard
1 tablespoon apple cider vinegar
¾ cup olive oil
2 tablespoons hot water
Salt and freshly ground black
  pepper to taste
1 cup grilled corn kernels
  (page 180)
1 teaspoon minced fresh chives

*Make the salad:* Combine all the greens, wash in cool water, and spin dry. Arrange leaves and onion rings on 4 individual salad plates.

*Make the vinaigrette:* Combine in a blender the chopped bell peppers, pimiento, mustard, and vinegar. Blend for 1 or 2 minutes until very smooth. Strain through a fine sieve. Return purée to blender and, with the motor running, add the oil slowly. Add the hot water, salt, and pepper. Pour and scrape the vinaigrette into a bowl, then add the grilled corn and chives. Set aside, covered, in the refrigerator until serving time.

*Cook the chicken:* On the grill, cook the chicken breasts to your liking, about 5 minutes a side. As soon as the breasts are removed from the grill, slice them very thin (about ¼ inch), and while they are still warm, place them in a fan shape on top of each plate of salad greens.

Spoon about ¼ cup of the Red Pepper and Grilled Corn Vinaigrette on top of the chicken salad.

# *Grilled Chicken Salad*

## WITH CHILI MAYONNAISE

*I love a good chicken salad. I've tried different ingredients, from daikon radishes to European cucumbers, but I always come back to this basic walnut, raisin, and apple combination. You can also make this salad with tuna or salmon. Great as a sandwich filling, or with sliced tomatoes and a basil vinaigrette. Grill some extra chicken at your next cookout and try it.*

**MAKES 4 SERVINGS**

*½ cup Chili Mayonnaise (page 240), or add ¼ teaspoon Tabasco to regular mayonnaise*
*4 boneless chicken breast halves (6 to 8 ounces each), grilled, chilled, and cut into ½-inch cubes*
*½ cup celery, chopped ¼ inch thick*

*¼ cup raisins*
*½ cup apple, cut into small cubes*
*¼ cup chopped walnuts*
*Salt and freshly ground black pepper to taste*
*2 cups chopped mixed greens*
*2 sliced tomatoes*

Make the Chili Mayonnaise (page 240). In a large glass bowl, combine the mayonnaise, chicken, celery, raisins, apples, walnuts, salt, and pepper. Mix well.

Serve on top of mixed greens with sliced tomatoes on the side.

# Pork Tenderloin and Couscous Salad

*T*he bright bits of peppers and vegetables in the couscous make this pretty salad look like confetti. If you have never tasted couscous, you should try it. Couscous is not a grain but actually a tiny cooked and dried pasta that needs only boiling water to rehydrate it. Couscous is available at most supermarkets.

**MAKES 4 SERVINGS**

### COUSCOUS SALAD
3 tablespoons olive oil, divided
¼ cup red onion, cut into ¼-inch cubes
¼ cup celery, cut into ¼-inch cubes
¼ cup red bell pepper, cut into ¼-inch cubes
¼ cup green bell pepper, cut into ¼-inch cubes
1 cup couscous
2 tablespoons unsalted butter
¼ teaspoon salt

½ teaspoon ground cinnamon
1½ cups water
¼ cup Calamata olives, pitted and chopped

### PORK TENDERLOIN
2 small pork tenderloins, 1½ to 2 inches in diameter, about 1½ pounds
¼ cup honey
½ cup orange juice
1 tablespoon unsalted butter
½ tablespoon olive oil

*Make the couscous:* In a heavy saucepan with a lid, heat 1 tablespoon of the olive oil. When the oil is hot, add the onion and cook until translucent, about 3 minutes.

Add the celery and bell peppers. Sauté for a few minutes until vegetables are bright in color and crisp-tender.

Add the couscous, butter, salt, cinnamon, and water. Bring to a boil. Remove from the heat, cover, and let stand for 10 minutes.

Fluff couscous lightly with a fork. Add the remaining olive oil and the olives. Mix well and reserve.

*Make the pork tenderloins:* Heat oven to 400°.

Stir together the honey and orange juice, and pour over the pork tenderloins. Heat the butter and olive oil in an ovenproof sauté pan or roasting pan on top of the stove. When hot, sear the tenderloins on all sides for about 2 minutes. Place in the oven and roast for 8 to 10 minutes.

Remove tenderloins and let rest for 5 minutes.

*To assemble the salad:* Spoon about 1 cup of Couscous Salad in the center of each plate. Cut the pork tenderloins into very thin, ¼-inch-thick slices. Fan out the pork slices from the center of the plate, with the pork slightly touching the couscous salad.

# Pasta and
# Rice

PENNE WITH CALAMATA OLIVES

GOAT CHEESE RAVIOLI WITH
PORT WINE SAUCE

TORTELLINI WITH PROSCIUTTO AND TOMATO SAUCE

SPAGHETTINI WITH LITTLENECK CLAMS

LINGUINE WITH SHRIMP, GREEN OLIVE,
AND TOMATO SAUCE

FETTUCCINE WITH SHRIMP PROVENÇALE

BLACK FETTUCCINE WITH FLORIDA LOBSTER

RIGATONI AND HERBED CHICKEN STRIPS

CINNAMON BROWN RICE

GARLIC AND BASIL BASMATI RICE

SAFFRON RISOTTO

RISOTTO WITH GINGER AND CARROT JUICE

SEAFOOD RISOTTO WITH TOMATO AND
BASIL JUICE

GOAT CHEESE POLENTA

# Penne with Calamata Olives

*Tangy, flavor-packed Calamata olives and mild, creamy goat cheese give this simple pasta dish a memorable richness. It's perfect for tossing together when friends drop in unexpectedly. Crusty bread and red wine are easy finishing touches.*

**MAKES 4 SERVINGS**

½ cup Calamata olives
2 tablespoons unsalted butter, divided
¼ cup minced yellow onion
2 tablespoons minced garlic
3 tablespoons chopped sun-dried tomatoes in oil
1 teaspoon fresh rosemary leaves, chopped

1 teaspoon fresh thyme leaves, chopped
½ cup dry white wine
½ cup Chicken Stock (page 233)
1 pound penne
Salt and freshly ground black pepper to taste
½ cup crumbled mild goat cheese

Pit and chop the Calamata olives. In a saucepan, heat 1 tablespoon butter, add the onion, cook until translucent, not brown, add the garlic. When the garlic becomes fragrant, add the sun-dried tomatoes and sauté for 1 minute. Add the rosemary, thyme, white wine, and olives. Reduce heat to low and let simmer until volume is reduced by half. Add the stock, and keep the pan on very low heat.

Meanwhile, cook the pasta until al dente. Drain well and return to the pot in which it was cooked. Add the remaining butter, salt, and pepper. Mix well. Add the olive sauce and cheese, and serve immediately.

# Goat Cheese Ravioli

## WITH PORT WINE SAUCE

*U*sing wonton skins to make ravioli is fun. You can prepare the ravioli ahead of time. Place in 1 layer on a baking tray, cover well, and refrigerate. Once you've tried this simple technique, you'll want to experiment with other fillings.

**MAKES 4 SERVINGS**

### RAVIOLI

2 ounces pancetta, finely diced

1 teaspoon minced garlic

8 ounces spinach leaves, washed
   and chopped

5 ounces mild crumbled goat
   cheese

¼ teaspoon salt

¼ teaspoon freshly ground black
   pepper

32 wonton skins, 3-inch size
   (available in supermarkets or
   Oriental markets)

1 egg yolk, beaten with
   1 tablespoon water

### PORT WINE SAUCE

3 tablespoons unsalted butter,
   divided

2 tablespoons minced shallots

⅓ cup pine nuts plus ¼ cup for
   garnish

2 cups port wine

1 cup Brown Beef Stock (page
   236)

2 sprigs fresh thyme

Salt and freshly ground black
   pepper

*Make the ravioli:* In a large nonstick skillet, cook the pancetta over medium heat until slightly crisp. Add the garlic and spinach leaves, and cook for about 2 minutes. The spinach will wilt and its volume reduce greatly.

Add the crumbled goat cheese, salt, and pepper, and toss to combine all ingredients. Set aside to cool.

Place 16 wonton skins on a work surface, such as the kitchen counter. Place 1 tablespoon of the spinach mixture in the middle of each square. Using a small paint brush or your fingertip, brush the egg wash around the edge, about ½ inch wide.

Put another wonton skin on top of each filled bottom and press firmly to close. Using a cookie cutter, a fluted cutter, or a knife, cut 2½-inch round circles and discard the excess wonton skin.

You may refrigerate the ravioli, covered, in a single layer on a baking tray.

Bring a potful of water to a boil. Cook the ravioli until they float to the top, approximately 1½ minutes. Drain and place on paper towels.

*Make the sauce:* In a saucepan, heat 1 tablespoon of the butter. Add the shallots and cook until they are translucent, about 3 minutes.

Add the ⅓ cup pine nuts and sauté for 2 minutes. Add the port and let boil gently until volume is reduced by half. Add the stock and thyme, and cook for 10 minutes.

Transfer to a food processor or blender and blend until very smooth. Strain through a fine sieve, then return mixture to a saucepan and bring to a boil.

Let reduce until ¾ cup remains. Add salt and pepper, taste, then adjust the seasoning. Remove from the heat and swirl in the remaining butter. Set aside until serving time.

To serve, spoon about 2 tablespoons of the Port Wine Sauce on the bottom of each plate, arrange 4 ravioli per plate, and sprinkle the remainder of the pine nuts all the way around the plate for garnish.

# Tortellini with Prosciutto and Tomato Sauce

*This* is one of The Left Bank's classic dishes. It is easy to prepare and the sauce is equally delicious with ravioli or plain noodles. The tomato purée and the cream create a beautiful pink sauce. Try different brands of tortellini to select your favorite.

**MAKES 4 SERVINGS**

1 tablespoon unsalted butter
¼ cup prosciutto, cut into ¼-inch cubes
1 tablespoon minced shallots
¼ cup vodka, optional
1½ cups peeled, seeded, and chopped tomatoes
2 tablespoons canned tomato purée

½ cup heavy whipping cream
1 pound cheese- or spinach-filled tortellini
Salt and freshly ground black pepper to taste
¼ cup freshly grated Parmigiano-Reggiano cheese

In a sauté pan, heat the butter and add the prosciutto and shallots. Sauté for 2 minutes, or until shallots turn light brown. Add the vodka, if using, and stir, then ignite with a match. When the flames subside, add the tomatoes, tomato purée and cream, and let reduce for 2 to 3 minutes.

Meanwhile, cook the tortellini following the package directions. As soon as you remove the tortellini from the water, add them to the sauce. Adjust the salt and pepper. Sprinkle with the Parmigiano-Reggiano cheese and serve immediately.

# Spaghettini with Littleneck Clams

*O*nce you've made this flavorful, fresh version of pasta with clams, you'll never settle for anything less. Discard any clams that remain closed after the others have opened their shells during cooking. Serve with warmed crusty rolls to soak up the juices. This recipe is easy to scale down for 1 or 2 people; to serve more than 4, cook the clams in 2 pots.

**MAKES 4 SERVINGS**

*1 pound fresh or dried spaghettini*
*2 tablespoons olive oil*
*48 littleneck clams*
*1 small onion, finely diced*
*1 tablespoon minced garlic*
*1 cup Chardonnay or dry white wine*

*½ cup peeled, seeded, and chopped tomatoes*
*1 tablespoon finely chopped fresh cilantro or parsley*
*Salt and freshly ground black pepper to taste*
*12 cilantro or parsley leaves, for garnish*

Bring a large pot of water to a boil and cook the pasta following the directions on the package. If you are using fresh pasta, be sure to wait until the last minute, as it cooks in just a few minutes.

In a large saucepan or Dutch oven, heat the olive oil over medium-high heat. Add the clams and onion and cook, stirring occasionally, until the clams begin to open, 5 to 10 minutes.

Add the garlic and when it is fragrant, in about 1 minute, add the wine. When the clams have opened completely, add the tomatoes and season with the chopped cilantro, salt, and pepper. Discard any clams that haven't opened their shells.

Divide the cooked spaghettini among individual soup plates. Arrange the clams all around the pasta and pour the sauce over it.

Garnish with cilantro leaves.

# Linguine with Shrimp, Green Olive, and Tomato Sauce

*U*se the shrimp shells to make a quick stock to add an essential depth of flavor to this colorful pasta dish. The stock doesn't take long to make, and it pays off in big taste. Try to find shrimp with the heads still on; the heads yield a lot of flavor.

**MAKES 4 SERVINGS**

**SHRIMP STOCK**
Shells, tails, and heads from
   1 pound large shrimp
   (21 to 25 per pound)
1 tablespoon olive oil
½ cup minced onion
½ cup minced carrots
½ cup minced celery
2 tablespoons minced shallots
½ cup Chardonnay or dry white
   wine
1 cup chopped fresh tomatoes
1 cup water

**SHRIMP, GREEN OLIVE, AND TOMATO SAUCE**
1 cup Shrimp Stock
1 tablespoon olive oil

1 pound large shrimp (21 to 25
   per pound), peeled and
   deveined (reserve shells,
   heads, and tails for stock; see
   above)
1 tablespoon minced garlic
½ cup green olives, pitted and
   chopped
1 cup peeled, seeded, and chopped
   tomatoes
Salt and freshly ground black
   pepper to taste
1 tablespoon chopped fresh sweet
   basil leaves
1 pound linguine

*Make the shrimp stock:* Peel and devein the shrimp and remove the tails. In a saucepan, heat the olive oil and add the shrimp shells and heads. Cook until bright pink. Add the onion, carrots, celery, and shallots, and sauté for about 3 minutes.

Add the wine and let boil gently until the volume is reduced by half. Add the tomatoes and water, then reduce the heat and let cook for 45 minutes. Strain through a fine sieve. There should be about 1 cup liquid. If there is more, return it to the saucepan and reduce until 1 cup remains.

*Make the pasta and sauce:* Bring a large pot of lightly salted water to a boil, and start the sauce.

Heat olive oil in a large sauté pan, then add the shrimp and sauté for 1 minute on each side. Add the garlic and cook until fragrant (about 1 minute), then add the olives and sauté for 4 minutes.

Add the tomatoes and sauté for 1 more minute. Add the Shrimp Stock and cook 1 minute. Season with salt, pepper, and basil.

Cook the linguine according to package directions, drain, and divide the pasta among individual dinner plates. Spoon the shrimp and sauce over the pasta, and serve immediately.

# Fettuccine with Shrimp Provençale

*The garlic, tomato, basil, and Pernod give this shrimp dish a traditional Provençal flavor. Make sure to have all of the ingredients ready before you begin to sauté them. Serve these wonderful fresh-tasting shrimp with buttered fettuccine mounded in the center of the plate.*

**MAKES 4 SERVINGS**

1 tablespoon olive oil
1 tablespoon unsalted butter
2 pounds jumbo shrimp (12 to 15 per pound), peeled and deveined
1 tablespoon finely minced garlic (about 2 cloves)
½ cup peeled, seeded, and chopped tomatoes
1 tablespoon Pernod liqueur

¼ cup dry sherry
1 teaspoon chopped fresh sweet basil leaves
1 teaspoon chopped fresh parsley
Salt and freshly ground black pepper to taste
2 tablespoons unsalted butter, optional
1 pound fettuccine noodles, cooked as directed on package

Heat the olive oil and butter in a large sauté pan over medium heat. When light brown and sizzling, add the shrimp in 1 layer and sauté for 2 minutes.

Turn the shrimp over and cook 2 more minutes. Add the garlic and when fragrant (only a few seconds), add the tomatoes, Pernod, and sherry. Cook 2 more minutes.

Stir in the basil and parsley, and season with salt and pepper. For a richer, creamier sauce, remove the pan from the stove and swirl in butter, if desired.

To serve, arrange a mound of buttered fettuccine noodles in the center of the plate, then surround it with the shrimp.

# Black Fettuccine with Florida Lobster

*I love this pasta dish made with black squid ink fettuccine, but you should feel comfortable serving the sauce with your favorite pasta. If Florida lobster is not available, you can substitute large shrimp or even scallops.*

**MAKES 4 SERVINGS**

2 tablespoons unsalted butter
1 pound lobster tail meat, cut into
   ½-inch pieces
2 shallots, minced
1 garlic clove, finely minced
½ cup dry sherry
1 cup tomatoes, peeled, seeded,
   and chopped

1 tablespoon minced fresh sweet
   basil leaves
Salt and freshly ground black
   pepper to taste
1 pound fresh squid ink fettuccine

In a sauté pan, heat the butter. When hot, add the lobster pieces. Cook on one side for 1 to 2 minutes. Add the shallots and when translucent, turn the lobster on the other side and cook for 1 minute. Add the garlic and when fragrant, add the sherry. Let reduce by half. Add the tomatoes, basil, and salt and pepper. Cook for 1 more minute.

Cook the fettuccine al dente in boiling water. Drain the water and return the fettuccine to the same pot. Add the sauce, mix well, and serve immediately.

# Rigatoni and Herbed Chicken Strips

*This is comfort food for the nineties—easy to prepare, good for you, and bursting with fresh herbal flavor. A great recipe to scale down and make just for yourself when you need a little pampering. Rigatoni are thick, hollow tubes of ridged pasta. If you can't find freshly made rigatoni, use dried pasta.*

**MAKES 4 SERVINGS**

1 tablespoon chopped fresh sweet
    basil leaves
1 tablespoon chopped fresh thyme
    leaves
1 tablespoon chopped fresh
    tarragon leaves
1 tablespoon chopped fresh chives
⅓ cup olive oil, divided

1 pound fresh rigatoni
1½ pounds boneless, skinless
    chicken breasts, cut into long,
    1-inch-wide strips
2 garlic cloves, peeled and finely
    minced
½ cup freshly grated Parmigiano-
    Reggiano cheese

Fill a large pot with water and place it over high heat. While the water is coming to a boil, combine the herbs and the olive oil (minus 1 tablespoon) in a food processor and process to combine.

When the water comes to a boil, add the rigatoni and cook until al dente—tender but still with a little firmness to the bite, following the package directions.

Meanwhile, in a large sauté pan, heat the 1 tablespoon olive oil, add the chicken strips, and cook for 3 minutes on each side. Add the garlic and cook until fragrant, about 1 minute, then add the herbed oil. Heat through for 1 minute, then toss in the drained, cooked pasta. Sprinkle with freshly grated cheese. Serve immediately.

**RICE**

# Cinnamon Brown Rice

*I love the look, texture, and flavor of perfectly cooked brown rice. Since brown rice retains its outer bran layer, which has a great deal of cellulose, it needs to cook longer than white rice, 45 to 50 minutes. This rice is a flavorful accompaniment to pork or chicken.*

**MAKES 4 SERVINGS**

3 tablespoons unsalted butter,
   divided
1 onion, chopped fine
1 cup brown rice
2 teaspoons ground cinnamon

1 teaspoon salt
1 teaspoon freshly ground white
   pepper
2¼ cups water

In a 3-quart saucepan, heat 1 tablespoon butter; when hot, add the onion. When the onion is translucent, add the brown rice and cinnamon. Add the salt, pepper, and water; bring to a boil. Reduce the heat to low, cover tightly, and cook until all water has been absorbed, 45 to 50 minutes. Add 2 tablespoons butter, fluff the rice with a fork, and serve.

# Garlic and Basil Basmati Rice

*Basmati rice has a wonderful aroma and a great flavor. Once you have made this recipe a couple of times, I promise that you won't return to plain rice. Texmati rice, a type of basmati, is excellent and widely available.*

**MAKES 4 SERVINGS**

1 cup uncooked basmati rice
2 cups water
½ teaspoon salt
1 tablespoon unsalted butter

½ cup finely minced white onion
2 tablespoons minced garlic
1 tablespoon minced fresh sweet
basil leaves

Put the rice in a fine sieve and wash it under cold running water for a few minutes until the water coming out of the sieve is clear.

Combine the water, rice, and salt in a medium saucepan with a lid. Bring to a boil over high heat, then lower heat and cover partially. Let cook for 10 minutes. Drain immediately and rinse under cold water to remove any excess starch.

Heat oven to 400°. Generously butter six 4-ounce ramekins or oven-proof baking cups.

Heat the butter in a sauté pan until sizzling. Add onion and cook until translucent, not brown, about 5 minutes. Add the garlic and basil, stir and cook until garlic is fragrant, about 1 minute. Add the rice and stir well to mix. Pack the rice into the ramekins. (You can refrigerate the rice, covered, at this point for a few hours.)

To serve, bake rice at 400° for 15 to 20 minutes. Carefully unmold each serving onto a plate and serve immediately.

# Saffron Risotto

*This beautiful golden-orange risotto appears on the menu in many fine Italian restaurants, usually as the partner to osso buco. I love to serve it in little mounds that I shape with two soup spoons, as for a quenelle. For a main-dish risotto, you can even add seafood or chicken tenderloin. Be patient in cooking risotto, and its taste will reward you.*

**MAKES 6 SIDE-DISH SERVINGS**

*1 cup Chardonnay or other dry white wine*
*10–15 threads sun-dried Spanish saffron*
*¼ cup (½ stick) unsalted butter*
*1½ tablespoons sunflower oil*
*¾ cup minced white onion*
*1 cup Arborio rice (no substitutions)*

*4½ cups Chicken Stock (page 233), heated to just below simmer*
*2 tablespoons unsalted butter, optional*
*½ cup freshly grated Parmigiano-Reggiano cheese*
*Salt and freshly ground black pepper to taste*

In a small saucepan over medium heat, combine the Chardonnay and the saffron and boil gently until ½ cup wine remains.

In a large, heavy saucepan, heat the butter and sunflower oil over medium heat. When hot, add the onion and cook until translucent, not brown, 3 to 4 minutes maximum.

Add the rice and mix well for about 3 minutes with a wooden spoon to make sure the rice is well coated with butter.

Add the reduced wine and stir well with the wooden spoon until all the wine has been absorbed.

Add the hot stock, ½ cup at a time, stirring constantly until each addition is absorbed. This will take 20 to 30 minutes.

Remove the saucepan from the heat and add the optional butter and the Parmigiano-Reggiano cheese, mixing until completely smooth. The risotto should be creamy, not runny. Season with salt and pepper, and serve.

See the Note under Risotto with Ginger and Carrot Juice (page 89).

# Risotto

## WITH GINGER AND CARROT JUICE

*If you have never made risotto, you must try this recipe (see* Note*). You can replace the carrot juice with any favorite vegetable juice, such as spinach or celery. Just experiment; it's fun and rewarding.*

**MAKES 6 SIDE-DISH SERVINGS**

**GINGER AND CARROT JUICE**
12–14 sweet fresh carrots, peeled
2 tablespoons minced fresh ginger
4 tablespoons unsalted butter

**RISOTTO**
¼ cup (½ stick) unsalted butter
1½ tablespoons sunflower oil
¾ cup minced white onion
1 cup Arborio rice
   (no substitutions)
1 tablespoon minced fresh ginger

½ cup Chardonnay or dry white
   wine
3½ cups Chicken Stock (page
   233), heated to just below
   simmer
¼ cup grated carrots
2 tablespoons unsalted butter,
   optional
½ cup freshly grated Parmigiano-
   Reggiano cheese
Salt and freshly ground black
   pepper to taste

*Make the ginger-carrot juice:* Juice the carrots and ginger; measure out 2 cups.

In a saucepan, heat the carrot juice and when lukewarm, add the butter, 1 tablespoon at a time. Mix well and set aside for later use.

*Make the risotto:* In a heavy saucepan, heat the butter and sunflower oil over medium heat. When hot, add the onion and cook until translucent, not brown, 3 to 4 minutes maximum.

Add the rice and ginger, and mix well for about 3 minutes with a wooden spoon to make sure all the rice is well coated with butter.

Add the wine and stir well with the wooden spoon until all the wine has been absorbed. Add the hot stock, ½ cup at a time, stirring constantly until each addition is absorbed. This will take 20 to 30 minutes.

Add 1 cup of ginger-carrot juice and the grated carrots, and stir; when the rice has absorbed the juice, it will be thoroughly cooked.

Remove the saucepan from the heat and add the optional butter and the Parmigiano-Reggiano cheese, mixing until completely smooth. The risotto should be creamy, not runny. Season with salt and pepper, and serve.

**NOTE:** Making risotto isn't difficult. Just get all the prep work done before you begin to cook and bring the stock to just below a simmer in a saucepan. Patiently stir in the stock a little at a time. The risotto will develop a creamy consistency, but each grain should have a distinct bite. Do not overcook the rice, as it will become sticky and very starchy. Arborio rice, with its stubby grains, is a must for perfect risotto; it is available in well-stocked supermarkets, gourmet stores, and Italian markets.

# Seafood Risotto

## WITH TOMATO AND BASIL JUICE

*This wonderful dish reminds me of a small restaurant in Rome where they used to serve a huge plate of seafood risotto, overflowing with mussels, clams, lobsters, and many other kinds of seafood. Serve this risotto with a fresh green salad and garlic bread. Be sure to prepare the seafood before you begin to cook the rice.*

**MAKES 4 SERVINGS**

### TOMATO AND BASIL JUICE
1½ pounds vine-ripened tomatoes
¼ cup chopped fresh sweet basil
    leaves
2 tablespoons unsalted butter, cut
    into pieces

### SEAFOOD
1 tablespoon unsalted butter
1 tablespoon olive oil
1 pound large shrimp (16 to 20
    per pound), peeled and
    deveined
½ pound sea scallops, 30 to 40
    per pound
1 teaspoon minced garlic
¼ cup Chardonnay or dry white
    wine

### RISOTTO
¼ cup (½ stick) unsalted butter
3 tablespoons olive oil
1½ cups minced white onion
1 tablespoon minced garlic
2 cups Arborio rice
    (no substitutions)
1 cup Chardonnay or dry white
    wine
8 cups Chicken Stock (page 233),
    heated to just below simmer
1 cup peeled, seeded, and chopped
    tomatoes
Salt and pepper to taste

*Make the juice:* Use your juicer (see Note) to make 2 cups of tomato juice with no seeds or skin.

Put the juice and the basil in a saucepan, and bring to a boil. Reduce heat to medium and cook until 1 cup remains. Strain through a fine sieve. Add the butter and stir to melt. Set aside until needed.

*Make the seafood mixture:* In a sauté pan, heat the butter and oil until very hot. Add the shrimp and sauté for 1 minute. Turn the shrimp, add the scallops, and sauté another 2 minutes.

Add the garlic and when fragrant, add the wine. Cook for a minute to reduce the liquid, then remove from heat, and reserve until ready to stir into the risotto.

*Make the risotto:* In a large, heavy saucepan, heat the butter and olive oil over medium heat. When hot, add the onion and cook until transparent (not brown), 3 to 4 minutes maximum.

Add the garlic and rice, and stir well with a wooden spoon to make sure all the rice is well coated with the butter, about 3 minutes.

Add the wine and stir, and cook until the wine is absorbed.

Now, start adding the stock, about ½ cup at a time, and stir until each addition is absorbed.

After all of the stock has been added, the rice should be almost cooked. Add the tomatoes, 1 cup of tomato-basil juice, and the seafood, and stir and cook a few minutes longer until the risotto is creamy, but not runny.

Season with salt and pepper. Serve immediately.

**NOTE:** If you do not have a juicer, put all ingredients in the blender, blend for about 1 minute. Strain through a fine sieve.

# Goat Cheese Polenta

*P*olenta is coarsely ground cornmeal that you cook in broth; it's available in "instant" forms, but you should really try the old-fashioned kind that takes about 30 minutes of stirring. It's not hard to make, and the taste payoff is tremendous. You can serve this polenta warm and soft right after cooking, but I like it best chilled in a ¾-inch layer in a baking pan, then cut into squares, and sautéed in a little butter and olive oil until crusty and golden brown.

**MAKES 8 SERVINGS**

4 cups Chicken Stock (page 233)
3 cups water
2 cups coarsely ground polenta
1 teaspoon salt
¼ teaspoon freshly ground white
  pepper

3 tablespoons unsalted butter
¼ cup heavy whipping cream
5 ounces mild goat cheese or a
  mild, blue Gorgonzola

In a large, heavy saucepan (preferably nonstick), combine the stock, water, and polenta, and whisk while bringing to a boil. Immediately reduce heat so that the mixture simmers gently. Stir almost constantly with a wooden spoon, scraping the bottom "corners" where the polenta may stick and burn.

Keep a close eye on the polenta, stirring at least every 5 minutes, while the polenta cooks for about 30 minutes.

Season with salt and pepper, and stir in the butter, cut into pieces, the cream, and the goat cheese. If the mixture seems too thick and heavy, add a little more cream. The polenta should pull away from the sides of the pot when it's done.

# Fish and Shellfish

COCONUT SOLE WITH ORANGE-LIME SAUCE

SAUTÉED HALIBUT WITH
AROMATIC VEGETABLES

CITRUS-ROASTED SALMON

PAN-SEARED MONKFISH WITH
SAFFRON AIOLI

SAUTÉED SALMON WITH CITRUS AND
CHILI SALSA

GRILLED SALMON WITH
PINK PEPPERCORN SAUCE

SAUTÉED RED SNAPPER WITH
PANCETTA SALSA

SUNSHINE RED SNAPPER WITH
PAPAYA BEURRE BLANC

NUT-CRUSTED RED SNAPPER IN MUSTARD AND
GINGER SAUCE

GRILLED MAHI-MAHI WITH AVOCADO SALSA

SAUTÉED MAHI-MAHI WITH GINGER AND LIME SAUCE

MARINATED SHRIMP AND SCALLOP KABOBS

ROASTED SWORDFISH WITH CHUNKY TOMATO AND
GARLIC SAUCE

GRILLED ORIENTAL SWORDFISH WITH
THREE-BEAN RELISH

PAN-SEARED TUNA WITH CUCUMBER AND MINT SAUCE

GRILLED YELLOWFIN TUNA WITH
PAPAYA-PINEAPPLE COMPOTE

BLUE CRAB CAKES WITH MANGO AND PAPAYA SAUCE

# Coconut Sole

## WITH ORANGE-LIME SAUCE

*You can make this recipe with chicken breasts using the same technique. Be sure to pound the breasts to about ¾-inch maximum thickness, or the shredded coconut will burn before the chicken is completely cooked.*

**MAKES 4 SERVINGS**

*1½ pounds sole fillets*
*Salt and freshly ground white*
  *pepper to taste*
*1 cup milk*

*½ cup all-purpose flour*
*2 beaten eggs*
*1 cup shredded coconut*
*2 tablespoons butter*

Season the sole fillets with salt and pepper. Dip the fillets in the milk, then very lightly dredge them in the flour. Dip the fillets into the beaten eggs, then into the coconut.

Heat the butter in a sauté pan large enough to hold the fillets without crowding. When hot, add the fish and cook about 1 to 1½ minutes on each side.

Serve immediately with 2 tablespoons of Orange-Lime Sauce.

**ORANGE-LIME SAUCE**
*¾ cup orange marmalade*
*½ cup Chicken Stock (page 233)*
*2 tablespoons lime juice*
*1 tablespoon Dijon mustard*

*4 dashes Tabasco sauce*
*1 tablespoon orange Curaçao,*
  *optional*
*Salt and freshly ground black*
  *pepper to taste*

Combine all ingredients and blend well.

# Sautéed Halibut

## WITH AROMATIC VEGETABLES

*The halibut is a firm, sweet, white-fleshed fish that needs a flavorful sauce to give it personality. It may seem like a lot of work to prepare this dish, but it is really not difficult. And after you have mastered the aromatic vegetable ragout, you can serve it with other fish or even a chicken dish.*

**MAKES 4 SERVINGS**

*2 tablespoons unsalted butter, divided*
*1 tablespoon olive oil*
*¼ cup minced red onion*
*¼ cup red bell pepper, cut into ¼-inch cubes*
*¼ cup green bell pepper, cut into ¼-inch cubes*
*¼ cup yellow bell pepper, cut into ¼-inch cubes*
*1 tablespoon finely minced Scotch Bonnet pepper*
*2 scallions, cut diagonally, ¼ inch thick*

*1 tablespoon minced garlic*
*¼ cup Chardonnay or other dry white wine*
*¼ cup clam juice*
*1 cup peeled, seeded, and chopped tomatoes*
*1 tablespoon chopped fresh sweet basil leaves*
*Salt and freshly ground black pepper to taste*
*4 6- to 8-ounce halibut fillets, 1 inch thick*

*Make the vegetables:* In a large sauté pan, heat 1 tablespoon butter and the olive oil. When hot, add the onion and cook until translucent, but not browned. Add the bell peppers, Scotch Bonnet pepper, and scallions. Sauté for 3 minutes.

Add the garlic. Sauté for 3 to 4 minutes at low heat. Be careful not to burn the garlic. Add the Chardonnay, clam juice, tomatoes, and basil. Add the salt and pepper, and cook for 5 minutes.

*Make the fish:* In another sauté pan on the stove top, add 1 tablespoon butter and when foamy, add the halibut. Sauté fish on one side for 4 to 5 minutes, turn over, cover, and cook for 5 more minutes.

Ladle the vegetables onto the plate and top with the halibut.

# Citrus-Roasted Salmon

*Tart-sweet citrus juices offer a perfect balance to the fatty richness of salmon. Try the technique with other fish, such as sea bass, or boneless chicken breasts.*

**MAKES 4 SERVINGS**

| | |
|---|---|
| 4 6- to 8-ounce salmon fillets | ¼ cup fresh grapefruit juice |
| 1 tablespoon unsalted butter | 2 tablespoons fresh lemon juice |
| 1 tablespoon olive oil | 2 tablespoons fresh lime juice |
| ¼ cup fresh orange juice | |

Heat oven to 375°. In a sauté pan large enough to hold the fillets without crowding, heat the oil and butter.

When hot, add the salmon and sauté for 1 minute, then turn on other side and add the combined fruit juices. Place the pan in the oven and bake for 8 to 10 minutes. The salmon should remain slightly translucent in the center.

Serve immediately. Excellent with basmati rice.

# Pan-Seared Monkfish

## WITH SAFFRON AIOLI

*I was first introduced to monkfish, also called belly fish, when I was working in a restaurant on the French Riviera. In France it is called* baudroie *and is used in traditional bouillabaisse. It is one of the ugliest sea creatures I have ever prepared, but only the tail section is used. The meat is snow-white and very delicate, delicious served with basmati rice.*

*Saffron aioli is a very delicious and addictive sauce that is perfect for many Mediterranean dishes. Be sure to buy superior-quality saffron (Spanish is my favorite). You can use the aioli for chicken or crabmeat salad, or as a condiment for hamburgers, french fries, hot dogs, or grilled chicken. Make the aioli before you cook the fish.*

**MAKES 4 SERVINGS**

**SAFFRON AIOLI**
*10 saffron threads*
*¾ cup Chardonnay or dry white wine*
*4 garlic cloves*
*¼ teaspoon salt*
*2 egg yolks*
*1 teaspoon Dijon mustard*
*1 cup extra-virgin olive oil*
*1 tablespoon white wine vinegar*
*1 teaspoon fresh lemon juice*
*¼ teaspoon freshly ground black pepper*

**MONKFISH**
*1 monkfish tail (approximately 2 pounds), skin removed*

*All-purpose flour for dredging*
*Salt and freshly ground black pepper to taste*
*1 tablespoon olive oil*
*2 tablespoons minced onion*
*1 teaspoon fennel seeds*
*1 tablespoon minced garlic*
*½ cup Chardonnay or dry white wine*
*5 saffron threads*
*1 cup peeled, seeded, and chopped tomatoes*
*1 tablespoon tomato purée*
*1 cup Chicken Stock (page 233)*
*1 tablespoon Pernod liqueur*

*Make the saffron aioli:* Combine the saffron and wine in a stainless steel saucepan, bring to a boil, and let bubble briskly until volume is reduced to ⅓ cup. Strain through a fine sieve into a small bowl and set aside.

Peel and chop the garlic very fine. With a mortar and pestle or the flat side of a large chef's knife, pound or crush the garlic with the salt into a paste. In a stainless steel bowl, whisk together the egg yolks, garlic, and mustard; then, whisking constantly, very gradually drizzle in the oil. The consistency should be like a thick mayonnaise. You may not need all of the oil. Add the vinegar, lemon juice, freshly ground black pepper, and saffron-wine reduction, and whisk gently. Makes about 1½ cups.

*Make the monkfish:* Cut the monkfish tail into scallopine approximately 1 inch thick. Lightly dredge each piece in flour, making sure to dust off excess flour, and salt and pepper each piece.

In a large sauté pan, heat the olive oil and when hot, add the fish. Sauté for 2 to 3 minutes, then turn over. Add onion and cook until translucent, not browned, then add the fennel seeds and garlic.

When the garlic becomes fragrant, add the wine and saffron. Let reduce by half, add the tomatoes, tomato purée, stock, and Pernod. Cook until the fish is cooked all the way through, approximately 7 to 8 minutes.

Spoon the broth onto the bottom of each plate and arrange the fish scallopine on top. Using a squeeze bottle (such as an empty mustard container), drizzle about 2 tablespoons of saffron aioli on top of each serving.

# Sautéed Salmon

## WITH CITRUS AND CHILI SALSA

*The heat of fresh chilies, the coolness of citrus, and the full taste of rich salmon make this a signature* Sunshine Cuisine *fish dish. Try it with bluefish, as well.*

*The combination of citrus, soy sauce, Dijon mustard, and olive oil create an indescribable taste sensation. Make sure to mix the citrus segments at the end of preparation so they retain their individual, delicate texture.*

**MAKES 4 SERVINGS**

### SALMON
4 6- to 8-ounce salmon fillets, cut
    on the diagonal ¾ inch thick
1 tablespoon unsalted butter
1 tablespoon sunflower oil
1 tablespoon chopped fresh chervil

### CITRUS AND CHILI SALSA
1 Scotch Bonnet pepper, sliced
    and seeded
1 tablespoon rice wine vinegar
1 tablespoon soy sauce
¼ teaspoon ground ginger
1 tablespoon Dijon mustard

1 tablespoon minced garlic
¼ cup orange juice
¼ cup grapefruit juice
½ cup olive oil
1 tablespoon cubed lime segments
    (see Note)
1 tablespoon cubed lemon
    segments
¼ cup cubed orange segments
¼ cup cubed grapefruit segments
1 tablespoon finely chopped fresh
    chervil
Salt and freshly ground black
    pepper to taste

*Make the salmon:* In a sauté pan large enough to hold the salmon without crowding, heat the butter and oil. When hot, add the salmon and sauté for 2 to 3 minutes. Turn and sauté 2 to 3 minutes on the other side. The fish should remain slightly translucent in the center.

*Make the salsa:* In a blender, place the Scotch Bonnet pepper, rice wine vinegar, soy sauce, ginger, mustard, garlic, and the orange and grapefruit juices. Blend well and, with the motor running, add the olive oil. Remove from the blender into a glass bowl and add the citrus cubes, the chopped chervil, salt, and pepper.

To serve, pour 2 tablespoons of the salsa into the bottom of 4 large white dinner plates. Place the salmon on top and sprinkle with the chervil.

**NOTE:** To prepare the citrus segments, peel and carefully remove the white parts and seeds of all the citrus. Cut the flesh into small ¼-inch cubes.

# Grilled Salmon
## WITH PINK PEPPERCORN SAUCE

*Nothing could be more delicious than simply grilled salmon, served with a rich sauce with a hint of rum.*

**MAKES 4 SERVINGS**

4 salmon fillets, 6 to 8 ounces
   each
2 tablespoons olive oil for
   brushing

**PINK PEPPERCORN SAUCE**
1½ tablespoons unsalted butter
2 tablespoons minced shallots
½ cup Chardonnay or other dry
   white wine

2 tablespoons dark rum
2 teaspoons pink peppercorns
1 tablespoon tomato paste
½ cup heavy whipping cream
Salt and pepper to taste

4 sprigs fresh dill, for decoration

Preheat the grill to high heat. Brush the salmon fillets with olive oil and let sit for 10 minutes. Meanwhile, make the sauce.

In a saucepan, heat the butter, and when bubbling, add the shallots. Cook until they are translucent, then add the wine and let reduce by half. Add the rum and ignite with a match. When flames subside, add the peppercorns, tomato paste, and cream. Let reduce until thick enough to coat the back of a spoon. Adjust seasoning with salt and pepper.

Grill the salmon for 3 minutes, then turn over and cook another 3 minutes.

To serve, pour 2 tablespoons sauce in the bottom of each plate, arrange the grilled salmon on top, and decorate with a sprig of fresh dill.

# Sautéed Red Snapper

## WITH PANCETTA SALSA

*R*ed snapper is one of the most abundant fish in the coastal waters of Florida. Be sure to buy the whole fish. This assures you that the fish is authentic red snapper, easily recognized by its red color and bright red eyes. You can prepare it with Ginger and Lime Sauce (page 110), Grapefruit and Dill Vinaigrette (page 112), or Pancetta Salsa. Pancetta is an unsmoked, rolled Italian bacon widely available in Italian specialty stores and large supermarkets. Or use a very high-quality ham or Canadian bacon.

**MAKES 4 SERVINGS**

### PANCETTA SALSA
3 thin slices pancetta or
   Canadian bacon, cut into
   small cubes
1 garlic clove, peeled and finely
   chopped
1 large shallot, peeled and minced
½ cup pitted and chopped Niçoise
   olives
½ cup peeled, seeded, and
   chopped tomatoes
1 cup extra-virgin olive oil
¼ cup rice wine vinegar

1 teaspoon minced fresh sweet
   basil leaves
1 teaspoon minced fresh parsley
Salt and freshly ground black
   pepper to taste

### FISH
4 6-ounce red snapper fillets
1 tablespoon unsalted butter
1 tablespoon olive oil
¼ teaspoon salt
¼ teaspoon freshly ground black
   pepper

*Make the salsa:* In a nonstick pan over very low heat, cook the pancetta or Canadian bacon until light brown in color. Add the garlic and shallot, and sauté for 1 more minute. Drain excess fat (Canadian bacon won't release much fat; pancetta will) and transfer sautéed mixture to a glass bowl.

Add the olives, tomatoes, oil, and vinegar, and mix well. Just before serving, season with the basil, parsley, salt, and pepper.

*Make the fish:* Heat oven to 375°. Heat the butter and oil over medium heat in a sauté pan large enough to hold the fillets without crowding, until the butter is light brown and sizzling. Place the fillets in the pan and cook for about 2 minutes.

Take the pan off the stove, turn the fish over, place the pan in the oven, and bake for 5 more minutes. Remove from pan and season immediately with salt and pepper.

Serve with Pancetta Salsa.

# Sunshine Red Snapper

## WITH PAPAYA BEURRE BLANC

*This is the first recipe I prepared for the pilot show of* Sunshine Cuisine *on WPBT in Miami. I was really concerned about the papaya I was using on the show; I was afraid that it would have no flavor or aroma. But I lucked out, as the papaya was probably one of the finest I have ever tasted. It must have been a good-luck papaya, because the show was the beginning of* Sunshine Cuisine.

**MAKES 4 SERVINGS**

**FISH**
*¼ cup cornmeal*
*¼ cup flour*
*4 8-ounce snapper fillets, skin removed*
*1 teaspoon unsalted butter*
*1 teaspoon olive oil*
*Salt and pepper to taste*

**PAPAYA BEURRE BLANC**
*1 stick (4 ounces) unsalted butter, divided*
*1 shallot, peeled and chopped*

*2 tablespoons Chardonnay wine vinegar*
*½ cup Chardonnay or other dry white wine*
*2 slices (about 8 ounces) ripe, flavorful papaya*
*3 tablespoons bourbon*
*½ cup heavy whipping cream*

*Papaya balls, carambola, and chives, to garnish (optional)*

Heat the oven to 375°.

*Make the fish:* Mix the cornmeal and flour in a pan or on a plate. Dip each snapper fillet in the mixture and dust off the excess.

In an ovenproof sauté pan large enough to hold the fillets without crowding, heat the butter and oil until light brown. (You may have to use 2 pans.) Add the snapper, salt and pepper to taste, and sauté for 1 minute. Turn the fillets, then place in the oven to bake for 4 to 5 minutes. When the fish is done, it will be opaque, not translucent.

*Make the Papaya Beurre Blanc:* In a saucepan, melt 2 tablespoons of the butter; add the shallot and sauté 1 minute until translucent. Add the vinegar and let reduce for 2 minutes. Add the wine and let bubble until reduced by half. Meanwhile, purée the papaya and bourbon in a blender. Add the wine and shallot mixture to the blender and blend again. Return the mixture to the saucepan, add the cream, and bring to a boil. Remove from heat and whisk in the remaining butter, a little at a time. The sauce will be glossy and thick.

Do not refrigerate or reheat this sauce; keep it at room temperature until serving, for a maximum of 2 hours.

*To serve:* Spoon about 2 tablespoons of sauce on each dinner plate and set the cooked fish in the middle. If desired, make papaya balls with a small melon cutter and arrange in the sauce. Slice some carambola (star fruit) and place slices around the rim of the plate. Add 4 or 6 chives, crisscrossed, on top of the fish. Enjoy the applause!

# Nut-Crusted Red Snapper
## IN MUSTARD AND GINGER SAUCE

*In this elegant dish, the ground nuts lend crunch to the soft, delicate snapper. Try this recipe using mahi-mahi or another favorite fish. Delicious served with tiny new potatoes, tossed with butter and chopped fresh cilantro.*

**MAKES 4 SERVINGS**

*4 tablespoons unsalted butter, divided*
*¼ cup finely ground pistachio nuts*
*¼ cup finely ground almonds*
*4 red snapper fillets (6 to 8 ounces each), 1 inch thick*
*1 tablespoon olive oil*
*¼ teaspoon white pepper*

**MUSTARD AND GINGER SAUCE**
*large shallot, peeled and finely minced*
*½ teaspoon minced fresh ginger*
*¼ cup Champagne or dry white wine*
*½ cup heavy whipping cream*
*1 teaspoon Dijon mustard*
*Salt and freshly ground white pepper to taste*

One hour before you start cooking, bring the butter to room temperature. Pulverize the nuts in a food processor until they are ground to the texture of granulated sugar; do not overprocess or the nuts will turn to butter. Dust the fillets with the nut flour.

In a nonstick sauté pan, heat 1 tablespoon of the butter and the olive oil, and sauté the fish over very low heat for about 3 minutes on each side, or until done.

Sprinkle with white pepper and remove the fillets to a warm platter.

In the sauté pan, add the minced shallot and sauté for 1 minute. Add the ginger and Champagne, bring the mixture to a boil, and lower the heat to medium. Add the cream and let reduce for 2 minutes. Reduce the heat to the lowest temperature and add the mustard and the remaining butter, 1 tablespoon at a time, stirring continuously. Add salt and pepper.

To serve, spoon about 3 tablespoons of sauce onto the bottom of each dinner plate. Place a snapper fillet on top of the sauce.

# Grilled Mahi-Mahi

## WITH AVOCADO SALSA

*I used Florida avocados for this recipe, but California avocados are also fantastic. You will find yourself eating the salsa by the spoonful. Serve it with your favorite poultry or with grilled shrimp.*

**MAKES 4 SERVINGS**

4 6- to 8-ounce mahi-mahi fillets
2 tablespoons olive oil
   for brushing

Preheat the grill to high heat. Brush the fish fillets with olive oil and let sit for 10 minutes. Meanwhile, make the salsa.

Grill the fish for 3 to 4 minutes on each side. To serve, pour 3 tablespoons of salsa on top of the fish. Decorate plate with cilantro leaves.

**AVOCADO SALSA**
2 cups perfectly ripe avocado,
   peeled and diced into
   ¼-inch cubes
½ cup finely diced red onion
1 cup peeled and seeded tomato
¼ cup extra-virgin olive oil
¼ cup lemon juice
¼ cup minced cilantro leaves
Salt and freshly ground black
   pepper to taste

In a stainless steel bowl, mix all ingredients carefully, so that avocados are not crushed.

# Sautéed Mahi-Mahi

## WITH GINGER AND LIME SAUCE

*M*ahi-mahi is a fast-swimming fish whose lean, flaky white flesh makes it a favorite. It's great eating. The recipe also works well with orange roughy. Have your fish market cut the fish pieces from fillets and make sure the dark center line is removed first. The fish pieces should be about 1 inch thick and 2 inches across. Measure all of the sauce ingredients into the food processor, but do not make the dressing until the fish is cooked.

**MAKES 4 SERVINGS**

### FISH
12 2-ounce scallopine of mahi-
    mahi
Flour for dredging
1 tablespoon sunflower oil
1 tablespoon unsalted butter
Salt and freshly ground black
    pepper to taste

### GINGER AND LIME SAUCE
1 teaspoon finely minced fresh
    ginger

2 tablespoons soy sauce
1 tablespoon Champagne vinegar
¾ cup sunflower oil
1 tablespoon freshly squeezed lime
    juice
Salt and freshly ground white
    pepper to taste
1 tablespoon hot Chardonnay or
    dry white wine

*Make the fish:* Heat oven to 400°. Dust the fish pieces lightly with flour and pat to remove excess.

In a nonstick, oven-proof sauté pan, heat the oil and butter. When light brown in color, add the fish and sauté for 2 minutes. Turn the mahi-mahi, then put the sauté pan in the oven and bake fish for 4 to 5 more minutes. It should be opaque throughout, not translucent; do not overcook it. Remove from the oven, sprinkle with salt and pepper, and place fish pieces on a serving plate.

*Make the sauce:* Combine all ingredients except the wine in a food processor and blend for 15 to 20 seconds. Add the hot wine and blend for 20 more seconds. Ladle on top of the sautéed mahi-mahi. Reserve the rest of the sauce for vegetables or rice.

# Marinated Shrimp and Scallop Kabobs

*T*he sweet pineapple juice in the mild marinade adds elusive flavor to beautiful kabobs of grilled seafood. The Grapefruit and Dill Vinaigrette is just tangy enough to complement the shrimp and scallops. I enjoy this fresh and fruity vinaigrette poured over a green salad, or with grapefruit segments or grilled chicken. If you are watching your cholesterol, omit the egg yolk.

**MAKES 4 SERVINGS**

**KABOBS**
1 pound jumbo shrimp
    (15 per pound)
½ pound large sea scallops
    (about 25 per pound)

**MARINADE**
1 cup olive oil
¼ cup apple cider vinegar
½ cup pineapple juice
1 sprig fresh rosemary
2 garlic cloves, peeled and
    cut in half
8 black peppercorns
1 small bay leaf

Juice of 1 lime
1–2 red Anaheim chilies, cut into
    1-inch squares (see Note)

**GRAPEFRUIT AND DILL
VINAIGRETTE**
1 egg yolk
Juice of 1 small lemon
1 tablespoon apple cider vinegar
2 tablespoons Dijon mustard
½ cup fresh-squeezed grapefruit
    juice
1 tablespoon fresh dill
1 cup extra-virgin olive oil
2 tablespoons hot water
Salt and freshly ground black
    pepper to taste

*Marinate the seafood:* Peel and devein the shrimp. Rinse the shrimp and scallops under cold running water, and let drain. Place in a glass dish and set aside.

Mix marinade ingredients together and pour over shrimp and scallops. Let stand at room temperature for 1 hour.

*Make the vinaigrette:* In a blender, combine the egg yolk, lemon juice, apple cider vinegar, Dijon mustard, grapefruit juice, and dill. Blend for 2 minutes.

Reduce speed and slowly pour in the olive oil. The mixture will thicken.

Add the hot water and blend 30 more seconds. Adjust the seasonings and serve. The vinaigrette will keep for a couple of days, covered, in the refrigerator.

*Make the kabobs:* Heat the grill or broiler on high heat.

Thread the shrimp, scallops, and pepper squares onto bamboo skewers, alternating each ingredient.

Grill or broil kabobs for 2 to 3 minutes a side. Be careful not to overcook! Serve immediately with the Grapefruit and Dill Vinaigrette.

**NOTE:** If Anaheim chilies are not available, substitute Hungarian sweet chili peppers or pimientos. Use red bell peppers only as a last resort.

# Roasted Swordfish

## WITH CHUNKY TOMATO AND GARLIC SAUCE

*The bright red and green of the tomato and basil add eye appeal to this dish. You can also serve the chunky sauce with grilled tuna or even chicken breast. This recipe can easily be adjusted to make 1 or 2 servings—or even 6 or 8.*

**MAKES 4 SERVINGS**

**FISH**
*4 swordfish steaks (about 8 ounces each), cut 1 inch thick*
*1 tablespoon olive oil*

**MARINADE**
*1 cup extra-virgin olive oil*
*3 large garlic cloves, peeled and cut in half*
*¼ cup white wine vinegar*
*8 whole black peppercorns*
*1 tablespoon finely chopped fresh sweet basil leaves*

**CHUNKY TOMATO AND GARLIC SAUCE**
*2 tablespoons olive oil*
*½ cup finely chopped white onion*
*3 cups peeled, seeded, and chopped tomatoes*
*Salt and freshly ground black pepper to taste*
*1 teaspoon finely chopped fresh thyme leaves*

*Marinate the fish:* Place the swordfish steaks side by side in a glass dish. Combine the marinade ingredients and pour over fish. Let stand at room temperature for 1 hour, or in the refrigerator for 4 to 5 hours.

*Cook the fish:* Heat oven to 375°.

Place olive oil in a large ovenproof skillet or roasting pan over medium heat on the stovetop. When the oil is hot, add the swordfish steaks and sear on one side for about 5 minutes.

Turn the fish over and place the pan in the oven. Let roast for 10 minutes.

*Make the sauce:* While the fish is roasting, make the sauce. In a medium saucepan, heat the olive oil, then add the onion. When the onion is translucent, about 5 minutes, add the tomatoes. Lower the heat and cook gently for 10 minutes. Season with salt, pepper, and thyme.

To serve, spoon the sauce onto a plate and place a swordfish steak on top of the sauce.

Serve with Garlic and Basil Basmati Rice (page 86).

# Grilled Oriental Swordfish

## WITH THREE-BEAN RELISH

*Swordfish is very lean, and if overcooked by only 60 seconds becomes dry. The marinade spiked with soy sauce and ginger will keep your steaks moist and flavorful. Grilled swordfish is one of the great pleasures of the table. The best recipes are the simplest ones. The Three-Bean Relish is an excellent accompaniment to grilled chicken or pork, as well as this swordfish.*

**MAKES 4 SERVINGS**

*4 swordfish steaks, 8 to 10 ounces
   each
Salt and freshly ground black
   pepper to taste*

**MARINADE**

*1 cup extra-virgin olive oil
2 garlic cloves, peeled and cut in
   half
1 teaspoon minced fresh ginger
2 tablespoons soy sauce
2 tablespoons lime juice*

Season the swordfish steaks with salt and pepper and place side by side in a glass dish. Combine the marinade ingredients and pour over the fish. Let sit at room temperature for 1 hour, or in the refrigerator for 4 to 5 hours.

Heat the grill to a medium-to-high heat. Spray a nonstick olive oil–flavored cooking spray on the grill. Grill the swordfish about 4 to 5 minutes on each side, or until cooked to your liking. Season with salt to taste.

Serve with Three-Bean Relish (page 186).

# Pan-Seared Tuna

## WITH CUCUMBER AND MINT SAUCE

*F*resh tuna has a completely different texture, color, and flavor than canned tuna. Have your fish market remove the mid-lateral strip of dark meat, which is bitter when you cook it. One of the most popular kinds of tuna is yellowfin, which has a medium-light color, not as white as albacore but not as dark as bluefin. When cooked medium rare to rare, the tuna steak remains moist, meaty, and tender. If overcooked even slightly, it is dry and tasteless. Grill the tuna, using this marinade. Cucumber and Mint Sauce provides a cool, fresh contrast to the rich tuna.

This sauce has a beautiful pale green color and an exciting fresh taste of fresh mint. Designed to accompany pan-seared tuna, the vinaigrette is equally good with grilled lamb. Use European, sometimes called seedless or English cucumbers; they're less watery. If unavailable, choose little Kirby or pickling cukes. As a last resort, you can use regular garden cukes, but peel them to remove the wax and add a little fresh parsley to the sauce to boost the color.

**MAKES 4 SERVINGS**

### MARINADE
4 large sprigs fresh mint,
   approximately ¼ cup, packed
1 cup extra-virgin olive oil
Juice of 1 lemon
Juice of 1 lime
1 tablespoon apple cider vinegar
8 black peppercorns

### FISH
4 8-ounce yellowfin tuna steaks,
   1 to 1½ inches thick
1 tablespoon olive oil

### CUCUMBER AND MINT SAUCE
1 large European cucumber,
   about 9 inches long and
   2 inches in diameter
1 tablespoon Dijon mustard
2 tablespoons fresh mint leaves
½ cup sunflower oil
2 tablespoons hot water
¼ teaspoon salt
¼ teaspoon pepper

*Marinate the tuna:* Bring a small saucepan of water to a boil, then drop in the mint leaves and let simmer for 10 seconds. Remove immediately.

Combine oil, lemon and lime juices, vinegar, and peppercorns in a glass bowl, then add the mint. Arrange the tuna steaks side by side in a shallow glass baking dish and pour the marinade over the fish.

Cover and let sit at room temperature for 1 hour.

*Make the sauce:* Cut the cucumber lengthwise into quarters, then slice off the seeds with a sharp knife. Do not peel. Reserve 1 cucumber quarter and cut the rest into chunks.

Place the cucumber chunks in a blender and add the mustard and mint. Blend for 1 minute. With the motor running, slowly pour in the oil, then the hot water, salt, and pepper. Blend well.

Pour into a serving or storage container. Thinly slice the reserved quarter cucumber into tiny triangles and stir into the sauce.

*Cook the tuna:* Heat 1 tablespoon oil in a large, heavy sauté pan. When very hot, add the tuna and sauté for 2 minutes on each side for medium rare.

Serve immediately with the Cucumber and Mint Sauce.

# Grilled Yellowfin Tuna

## WITH PAPAYA-PINEAPPLE COMPOTE

*This combination of flavors will not only complement the meaty, moist tuna, but each ingredient will stand on its own. Prepare everything in advance and grill the tuna at the last minute. Buy fresh fish; touch it to make sure it is firm and has no odor. And do not overcook it. I like to marinate my tuna 1 hour before I grill it, as it adds flavor and helps retain its moisture.*

**MAKES 4 SERVINGS**

### FISH
4 8-ounce yellowfin tuna steaks,
    about 1 to 1½ inches thick
Salt and freshly ground black
    pepper to taste

### MARINADE
1 cup extra-virgin olive oil
¼ cup soy sauce
2 large garlic cloves, peeled and
    cut in half
Juice of 1 lemon
Juice of 1 lime
¼ cup red wine vinegar
1 shallot, peeled and minced
8 black peppercorns
1 small bay leaf
1 teaspoon minced fresh ginger

### PAPAYA-PINEAPPLE COMPOTE
1 tablespoon olive oil
1 cup finely chopped red onion

1 medium green bell pepper,
    cored, seeded, and cut into
    ½-inch cubes
1 medium red bell pepper, cored,
    seeded, and cut into ½-inch
    cubes
1 teaspoon finely minced fresh
    ginger
2 garlic cloves, peeled and minced
1 jalapeño pepper, seeded and
    minced
½ cup apple cider vinegar
3 tablespoons soy sauce
1 cup pineapple, cut into ½-inch
    cubes
1 cup papaya, cut into ½-inch
    cubes
Juice of 1 fresh lime
½ cup firmly packed brown sugar

*Marinate the tuna:* Place the tuna steaks in 1 layer in a glass dish and season with salt and pepper. Combine marinade ingredients and pour over the tuna. Let marinate at room temperature for 1 hour.

*Make the compote:* Heat the olive oil in a heavy, medium-size, nonreactive pot, such as stainless steel, over medium heat; do not use an aluminum pan. Add the onion, bell peppers, and ginger, and cook, stirring frequently, until the onion is translucent. Add the garlic; when it is fragrant, stir in the jalapeño pepper, vinegar, and soy sauce along with the pineapple and papaya cubes, lime juice, and brown sugar.

Bring to a simmer, then reduce heat to very low and cook for 30 minutes, stirring to prevent sticking or burning. Serve warm or at room temperature.

*Grill the tuna:* Heat the grill or preheat the broiler. Spray the grill rack or broiler pan with olive-oil–flavored nonstick cooking spray. Remove the fish from the marinade and season with salt and freshly ground black pepper. Grill or broil 3 to 5 minutes on each side for medium rare.

Serve with Papaya-Pineapple Compote.

# Blue Crab Cakes

## WITH MANGO AND PAPAYA SAUCE

*This is a perfect dinner party appetizer. You can prepare everything in advance. Refrigerate the crab cakes and the Mango and Papaya Sauce. The crab cakes take only 5 minutes to cook. Lump crabmeat is the highest quality sold in seafood markets and the most expensive at about $20 a pound. You can economize and choose a lesser grade. Do not use canned crabmeat.*

*The sauce is perfect with crab cakes because it has enough fruit and flavor on its own, yet does not overpower the delicate flavor of the crab. You could also serve it with gently sautéed breast of chicken, or eat it by itself with a big soup spoon (as I do)!*

**MAKES 4 SERVINGS**

### CRAB CAKES
*1 tablespoon olive oil*
*1 large onion, peeled and finely chopped*
*2 celery stalks, finely chopped*
*2 large egg yolks*
*1 teaspoon Dijon mustard*
*1 tablespoon fresh lemon juice*
*¼ cup chopped fresh Italian parsley*
*¼ teaspoon Tabasco sauce*
*½ cup mayonnaise (preferably homemade)*
*1 pound cooked crabmeat, picked over for shells and cartilage*
*½ cup fresh bread crumbs*
*Salt and freshly ground black pepper to taste*
*½ cup dry bread crumbs*
*1 tablespoon unsalted butter, divided*

### MANGO AND PAPAYA SAUCE
*1 cup peeled ripe papaya, diced*
*1 cup peeled ripe mango, diced*
*4 sprigs fresh cilantro, chopped*
*1 teaspoon sugar*
*1 teaspoon balsamic vinegar*
*¼ teaspoon salt*
*1 tablespoon bourbon, optional*
*¼ teaspoon very ripe habanero pepper (see* Note)
*¼ cup Chardonnay or dry white wine*

*Make the crab cakes:* Heat the oil in a small frying pan over low heat. Add the onion and celery, and sauté until the onion is translucent (not brown), about 5 minutes. Remove from heat and let cool completely.

In a large stainless steel bowl, combine the egg yolks, mustard, lemon juice, Italian parsley, Tabasco, and mayonnaise, and mix thoroughly. Add the crabmeat and fresh bread crumbs, plus salt and pepper. Refrigerate the mixture for at least 3 to 4 hours.

Shape mixture into 6 to 8 patties, about ½ inch thick. Spread the dry bread crumbs on a plate or baking sheet and coat each crab cake lightly on both sides. Place crab cakes on a baking sheet lined with waxed paper and refrigerate for at least 2 hours, but not longer than 24 hours.

*Make the sauce:* Place all ingredients in a food processor and blend until very smooth. Strain the sauce through a fine sieve and hold in a covered container in the refrigerator until ready to use.

*Cook the crab cakes:* To cook, heat 1 teaspoon of butter in a nonstick frying pan and sauté the crab cakes over medium-low heat until a light golden brown, about 2 to 3 minutes on each side. Do not crowd the pan. Use about 1 teaspoon of butter per batch.

Serve with Mango and Papaya Sauce.

**NOTE:** I like habanero peppers' intense heat and tropical fruit flavor. It is best to wear rubber gloves when cutting chilies. Do not touch your face and be sure to wash your hands thoroughly when you are finished. If you cannot find habanero peppers, substitute Scotch Bonnet or any other fresh, hot chili pepper. You can substitute peaches and/or pineapple for any of the fruit.

# Poultry

Arroz con Pollo

Roasted Free-Range Chicken Stuffed with
Garlic-Herb Cheese

Roasted Chicken Breasts with
Red Bell Pepper Sauce

Grilled Chicken Breast with
Papaya and Avocado Sauce

Gingered Chicken Breasts

Mustard-Glazed Roast Chicken

Sautéed Chicken Breast
with Niçoise Vinaigrette

Roasted Peppers and Chili Sabayon Sauce
for Chicken

Grilled Chicken Breast with
Calamata Olive Sauce

Grilled Duck Breast with Olive and Chili Sauce

Roast Duck with Prune and Mango Sauce

Black Cherry, Pearl Onion, and Kirsch Sauce
for Duck

Honey-Glazed Roast Duck

Turkey Breast with Wild Mushrooms

# Arroz con Pollo

*Arroz con pollo (rice with chicken) is probably one of the most popular chicken dishes in South Florida. You can see it on almost every menu in Miami restaurants. If saffron is not available, substitute Bijol (ground annatto seed).*

**MAKES 4 SERVINGS**

*2 tablespoons olive oil
3 pounds chicken, cut into
   8 pieces
1½ cups chopped Spanish onion
1 green bell pepper, cut into
   ½-inch cubes
2 garlic cloves, minced
1 cup peeled, seeded, and chopped
   tomatoes
1 bay leaf*

*1 teaspoon freshly chopped
   oregano leaves
10 saffron threads
½ cup dry white wine
1 cup long-grain rice
2 cups Chicken Stock (page 233)
1 12-ounce package frozen green
   peas (cooked per package
   directions)
1 small jar pimientos, for garnish*

Preheat oven to 375°.

In a large, ovenproof kettle or Dutch oven, heat the olive oil. When hot, sauté the chicken until golden brown on all sides. Remove from pan and set aside.

Add the onion to the kettle and when translucent, add the bell pepper and garlic. When the garlic becomes fragrant, add the tomatoes, bay leaf, oregano, saffron, and white wine. Cook for 5 minutes. Add the rice, mix well, add the stock, and reserved chicken pieces. Cover and bake in the oven for approximately 20 minutes.

Garnish with the peas and pimientos.

# Roasted Free-Range Chicken

## STUFFED WITH GARLIC-HERB CHEESE

*A* rich, aromatic garlic-herb cheese blankets the roast chicken, infusing it with flavor and keeping the flesh moist and tender. You could also use a prepared herb cheese, such as Boursin. This chicken is wonderful served with a good Châteauneuf-du-Pape or a Clos du Bois Marlstone from California.

**MAKES 4 SERVINGS**

**GARLIC-HERB CHEESE**
2 large garlic cloves, peeled
1 tablespoon fresh sweet basil
　　leaves
1 teaspoon fresh thyme leaves
1 teaspoon fresh rosemary leaves
1 tablespoon fresh parsley
2 tablespoons almonds

¼ cup heavy whipping cream
16 ounces cream cheese

**CHICKEN**
1 3½- to 4-pound free-range
　　chicken (see Note)
2 tablespoons olive oil
1 tablespoon unsalted butter,
　　melted

*Make the garlic-herb cheese:* In a food processor fitted with a steel blade, process the garlic, basil, thyme, rosemary, parsley, almonds, and cream until finely chopped. Add the softened cream cheese (see Note) in chunks, and process to blend. Use a rubber spatula to scrape the mixture into a bowl and set it aside.

*Make the chicken:* Heat oven to 400°.

Remove any excess fat from inside the chicken and rinse the bird under cold running water. Pat dry with a paper towel. Starting at the neck, work your fingers under the skin to loosen it, moving back to the leg, all the way to the drumstick. (Avoid tearing the skin with your fingernails.) Once the skin is loosened, again use your fingers to spread an even layer, ¼ to ½ inch thick, of the garlic-herb cheese between the skin and the flesh of the chicken.

Salt and pepper the inside of the chicken, then stuff it with some of the remaining cheese (about ½ to 1 cup) (see Note). Season the outside of the chicken with salt and pepper, and brush with a mixture of olive oil and melted butter. Place the chicken on a rack in a foil-lined roasting pan in the middle of the oven and roast for 45 minutes, or until golden brown.

**NOTE:** Free-range chickens, which are allowed to "range" in a pasture and not kept in a cage, have better flavor and texture than regular roasters; they are available in specialty poultry markets and some large supermarkets. Or just use a regular chicken.

To soften the cream cheese quickly, unwrap it, cut it into large chunks, and place it on a microwave-safe plate. Microwave at 50 percent power for 30 seconds.

If you don't think you'll use all of the cheese mixture to stuff the chicken, divide it before stuffing. Then, you won't contaminate the cheese with any bacteria from the chicken.

# Roasted Chicken Breasts

## WITH RED BELL PEPPER SAUCE

*I like new and interesting ways to prepare chicken breasts. This is my latest creation I discovered by accident when the only vegetables I had on hand were bright red bell peppers. The touch of mustard and Chardonnay in the Red Bell Pepper Sauce makes this a very tasty dish.*

**MAKES 4 SERVINGS**

### CHICKEN
1 tablespoon sunflower oil
1 teaspoon unsalted butter
4 6- to 8-ounce chicken breast
   halves, skinned and boned

### RED BELL PEPPER SAUCE
1 tablespoon unsalted butter
2 large shallots, peeled and finely
   chopped

2 tablespoons white wine vinegar
¼ cup Chardonnay or dry white
   wine
1 large red bell pepper, cored,
   seeded, and chopped
1 egg yolk
1 tablespoon Dijon mustard
2 tablespoons unsalted butter,
   melted

Preheat oven to 375°.

*Make the chicken:* Place a roasting pan or other ovenproof pan on the stove, and heat the oil and butter until golden. Arrange the chicken in the pan without crowding and sauté for 3 minutes. Turn the chicken over, place the pan in the oven, and roast on the middle rack for 8 to 10 minutes, or until cooked.

*Make the sauce:* In a sauté pan, heat 1 tablespoon butter. Add the shallots and cook until translucent. Add the vinegar and let reduce by half. Add the white wine and let reduce by half again. Add the bell pepper and sauté for 3 to 4 minutes.

Transfer the sauce to a blender or food processor and blend well. With the motor running, add the egg yolk, mustard and melted butter, and blend well.

*To serve:* Spoon 2 tablespoons of sauce onto the bottom of each dinner plate and place a chicken breast on top.

# Grilled Chicken Breast

## WITH PAPAYA AND AVOCADO SAUCE

*This sauce is beautiful, fragrant, and delicious. Make it first, then grill the chicken. If papayas are not available, substitute mangoes or peaches. Serve 1 breast per person with 1 big spoonful of sauce next to the chicken and some rice, if you wish.*

**MAKES 4 SERVINGS**

4 6- to 8-ounce chicken breast
   halves, skinned and boned

**MARINADE**
½ cup Chardonnay, or dry white
   wine
⅓ cup olive oil
¼ cup soy sauce
2 tablespoons apple cider vinegar
1 Spanish onion, peeled and
   roughly chopped
2 tablespoons finely chopped fresh
   cilantro leaves

**PAPAYA AND
AVOCADO SAUCE**
½ cup Chicken Stock (page 233)
¼ teaspoon ground cinnamon
¼ teaspoon freshly grated nutmeg
1½ cups ripe papaya, cut into
   ¼-inch cubes
1 cup ripe avocado, cut into
   ¼-inch cubes
Salt and freshly ground black
   pepper to taste
1 tablespoon finely chopped fresh
   cilantro leaves

*Marinate the chicken:* Combine the marinade ingredients, then pour over chicken breasts in a shallow glass baking dish. Let sit at room temperature for about 1 hour, then cover and refrigerate at least 4 to 5 hours, or overnight.

*Make the sauce:* In a stainless steel saucepan, heat the stock and let boil gently until reduced by half. Stir in the cinnamon, nutmeg, and papaya. Cook and stir for 1 minute, just enough to warm the papaya slightly. Season with salt and pepper; stir in the cilantro. Set aside.

*Cook the chicken:* Grill the chicken about 4 to 6 minutes on each side over medium coals. Serve with the sauce over rice.

# Gingered Chicken Breasts

*M*ake this fresh and tangy sauce before you cook the chicken, because that takes only minutes. The sauce is wonderful also with meaty grilled swordfish or tuna. Served with fresh green snap peas this dish really is wonderful.

**MAKES 4 SERVINGS**

**GINGER AND LIME SAUCE**
1 tablespoon sunflower oil
2 large shallots, peeled and
　minced
⅓ cup rice wine vinegar
1 cup Chardonnay or dry white
　wine
½ cup Chicken Stock (page 233)
2 tablespoons finely chopped
　fresh ginger
3 sprigs fresh thyme
1 tablespoon soy sauce

1 tablespoon fresh lime juice,
　divided
Salt and freshly ground black
　pepper to taste
Finely grated zest from 1 green
　lime, divided
2 tablespoons unsalted butter

**CHICKEN**
1 tablespoon sunflower oil
1 teaspoon unsalted butter
4 6- to 8-ounce chicken breast
　halves, skinned and boned

*Make the sauce:* Heat the oil in a stainless steel saucepan, then add the shallots, and sauté until translucent. Add the vinegar and let bubble until the liquid is almost evaporated. Add the wine and stock, and lower heat to medium. Stir in the ginger, thyme, and soy sauce, and let cook until approximately ¾ cup remains. Strain the sauce through a fine sieve. Add half the lime juice, a little salt and pepper, and half the lime zest. Off the heat add the butter, 1 tablespoon at a time. Taste the sauce and add a little more lime juice and zest if you prefer it tangier.

Preheat the oven to 375°.

*Cook the chicken:* Place a roasting pan (or any ovenproof pan) on the stove and heat the oil and butter over medium-high heat until golden. Arrange the chicken in the pan without crowding and sauté for 3 minutes. Turn the chicken over and put the pan in the oven on the middle rack and roast for 8 to 10 minutes, or until cooked.

*To serve:* Spoon 2 tablespoons of sauce onto the bottom of each dinner plate and place a chicken breast on top. Serve with fresh snap peas.

# Mustard-Glazed Roast Chicken

*Here's a flavorful roast chicken that's quick and easy enough to serve for a weeknight family dinner—but only if you are a family of mustard lovers. Des Meaux mustard has whole mustard seeds in it.*

**MAKES 4 SERVINGS**

1 3½- to 4-pound free-range
    chicken
Salt and freshly ground black
    pepper to taste
4 sprigs fresh rosemary

**MUSTARD GLAZE**
1 tablespoon honey
2 tablespoons Des Meaux mustard
¼ cup orange juice
½ teaspoon ground cloves
½ teaspoon ground cinnamon
Salt and freshly ground black
    pepper to taste

Heat oven to 350°.

Remove any excess fat from inside the chicken and rinse the bird under cold running water. Pat dry with a paper towel.

Rub the inside of the chicken with salt and pepper. Combine the ingredients for the mustard glaze and use a pastry brush to apply it liberally to the outside of the chicken.

Place the sprigs of rosemary in the neck and body cavities of the chicken and under each wing. Place the chicken on a rack in a foil-lined roasting pan in the middle of the oven and cook for about 1 hour, or until golden brown and the juices run clear when the chicken is pricked with a knife.

If the chicken browns too fast, cover it with aluminum foil to continue cooking without burning the skin.

The last 5 minutes, brush more mustard glaze all over the bird and increase the heat to 450°, to ensure a deep golden-brown color.

# Sautéed Chicken Breast

## WITH NIÇOISE VINAIGRETTE

*O*nce you've used this adaptable technique a few times, it will become a standby in your kitchen. Chicken breasts are incredibly versatile, and I love to prepare them with different sauces. Here I share with you a Niçoise Vinaigrette (page 133) and a Roasted Peppers and Chili Sabayon Sauce (page 134). The Banana-Citrus Vinaigrette on page 30 would be good, too.

**MAKES 4 SERVINGS**

4 chicken breast halves, skinned
  and boned
1 tablespoon olive oil

1 garlic clove, peeled and finely
  chopped
¼ cup Chicken Stock (page 233)
½ cup Niçoise Vinaigrette
  (page 133)

In a large sauté pan over medium-high heat, warm the olive oil, then add the chicken and sauté on one side for 6 to 7 minutes.

Turn the chicken over and cook for 4 to 5 more minutes. Add the garlic, and when fragrant, add the stock and let reduce for 2 minutes.

If you use the Roasted Peppers and Chili Sabayon Sauce, top each chicken breast with 2 tablespoons of sauce. If you choose the Niçoise Vinaigrette, place 2 tablespoons on the bottom of each dinner plate, then place a chicken breast on top.

### Niçoise Vinaigrette

**MAKES ABOUT 2 CUPS**

*3 thin slices pancetta or
 Canadian bacon, cut into
 small cubes*
*1 large shallot, peeled and minced*
*1 garlic clove, peeled and finely
 chopped*
*½ cup pitted and chopped black
 olives*
*½ cup peeled, seeded, and
 chopped tomatoes*

*1 cup extra-virgin olive oil*
*¼ cup rice wine vinegar*
*Salt and freshly ground black
 pepper to taste*
*1 teaspoon minced fresh sweet
 basil leaves*
*1 teaspoon minced fresh parsley*

In a nonstick pan over very low heat, cook the pancetta or Canadian bacon until light brown in color. Add the shallot and garlic, and sauté for 1 more minute. Drain excess fat and transfer to a glass bowl. Stir in the olives and tomatoes, then add the oil, vinegar, salt, and pepper. Mix well. Just before serving, add the basil and parsley.

# Roasted Peppers and Chili Sabayon Sauce

*A savory sabayon sauce is a luscious accompaniment to plain grilled meat, fish, or chicken. Roasted red peppers add a beautiful color and a rich, deep flavor. Whisk the sauce vigorously over simmering water for best results. It takes just a few minutes to make a sabayon.*

**MAKES ABOUT 1 CUP**

1 red bell pepper
1 red pimiento
1 red jalapeño pepper
4 egg yolks
5 dashes Tabasco sauce

¼ cup Chardonnay or dry white
    wine
Salt and freshly ground white
    pepper to taste

Roast the bell pepper, the pimiento, and the jalapeño pepper (page 10). Seed and chop very fine.

In the top of a double boiler, whisk together the egg yolks, Tabasco sauce, and wine. Whisk constantly until the mixture quadruples in volume, 4 to 5 minutes. Add the salt, pepper, and chopped peppers. Remove from heat, then remove top of double boiler from bottom.

# Grilled Chicken Breast

## WITH CALAMATA OLIVE SAUCE

*This flavorful chicken marinates in a bright green paste of cilantro and garlic, then it is grilled. While you're waiting for the grill to heat, make the sauce, so it's ready when the chicken is. This is good made with chicken thighs, too.*

**MAKES 4 SERVINGS**

4 10-ounce chicken breast halves,
  bones and skin intact

**MARINADE PASTE**
4 garlic cloves, peeled
1 tablespoon white wine vinegar
¼ cup olive oil
½ cup fresh cilantro leaves

**CALAMATA OLIVE SAUCE**
1 tablespoon olive oil
1 garlic clove, peeled and chopped
  very fine

⅓ cup dry sherry
2 cups peeled, seeded, and
  chopped tomatoes
½ cup Chicken Stock (page 233)
¼ cup Almond Pesto (page 242),
  optional
⅓ cup pitted, chopped Calamata
  olives
Salt and pepper to taste
1 tablespoon chopped fresh parsley

*Marinate the chicken:* In a mini-food processor or blender, combine the garlic, vinegar, olive oil, and cilantro into a fine paste. Rub the paste all over the chicken, place in a glass baking dish, cover, and refrigerate at least 4 to 5 hours. Remove from the refrigerator about 1 hour before grilling.

*Make the sauce:* Heat the olive oil in a stainless steel saucepan and add the garlic. When the garlic is fragrant (30 to 45 seconds), add the sherry, tomatoes, stock, pesto (if using), and olives. Stir and cook over medium heat for 2 to 3 minutes. Season with salt and pepper, and add the parsley. Remove from the heat and hold until chicken is cooked.

*Grill the chicken:* Let any excess marinade drip away. Over a medium grill, cook the breasts, skin side up, for 5 to 7 minutes. Turn the chicken and grill 7 more minutes. Turn again, so skin side is up, and cook for 3 to 4 more minutes. Turn once more and finish grilling until chicken is cooked all the way through. The juice should be almost clear when you stick a small knife into the thickest part of the breast.

# Grilled Duck Breast

## WITH OLIVE AND CHILI SAUCE

*If you have eaten grilled duck breasts only in a restaurant, you'll be amazed at how easy they are to make at home. Ask your butcher to special-order the duck breasts for you; it's worth the effort. The Olive and Chili Sauce is beautifully intense with the olives adding a rich Mediterranean flavor.*

**MAKES 4 SERVINGS**

8 skinless and boneless duck
  breast halves

**MARINADE**
½ cup peanut oil
1 tablespoon sherry wine vinegar
2 tablespoons dry sherry
2 tablespoons soy sauce
1 tablespoon minced fresh ginger
1 bay leaf

**OLIVE AND CHILI SAUCE**
1 tablespoon olive oil
2 tablespoon unsalted butter,
  divided

1 large shallot, peeled and minced
3 garlic cloves, peeled and minced
2 tablespoons sherry vinegar
¼ cup dry sherry
¼ cup port wine
¼ cup Calamata olives, pitted
  and sliced
¼ cup green California olives,
  pitted and sliced
2 scallions, cut into ¼-inch
  diagonal slices
¼ cup peeled, seeded, and
  chopped tomatoes
1 small pimiento or red poblano
  chili pepper

*Marinate the duck:* Combine all the marinade ingredients and set aside a few spoonfuls for basting. Place the duck breasts in a shallow glass baking dish and pour the remaining marinade over them. Let sit at room temperature for about 1 hour, then cover and refrigerate at least 3 to 4 hours, or overnight.

*Make the sauce:* In a saucepan, heat the olive oil and butter. When hot, add the shallot and cook until translucent, about 3 minutes. Add the garlic and cook until fragrant—do not burn.

Add the vinegar and let bubble until volume is reduced by half. Add the wines and let boil gently until volume is reduced by half again.

Add the olives and cook for 5 minutes at low temperature. Remove from heat and add the scallions, tomatoes, chili pepper, and the remaining butter.

Stir until butter is melted and set aside until serving time.

*Grill the duck:* Preheat the grill to high heat. Grill the duck breasts until medium rare, 2 to 3 minutes on each side. Brush with the reserved marinade as they cook. Serve immediately, with Olive and Chili Sauce on the side.

# Roast Duck

## WITH PRUNE AND MANGO SAUCE

*D*uck preparation isn't quick. First, you must roast the duck, then make the stock, then make a delicious sauce. But it's worth the trouble. Spread the work over two days—prepare the duck and stock the first day, then finish with your choice of sauce on the day the duck will be served.

**MAKES 2 SERVINGS**

1 4½- to 5-pound Long Island
    duckling, fresh or frozen
Salt and freshly ground black
    pepper to taste
1 green apple, cut into cubes

1 orange, cut into quarters
1 sprig fresh rosemary
1 sprig fresh thyme
1 large onion, peeled and cut into
    8 pieces

If the duckling is frozen, thaw it slowly in the refrigerator, allowing at least 24 hours to defrost it, but 48 hours is better. Do not use the running-water method, as the meat becomes tough and dry later during cooking if you rush the defrosting. Use fresh, unfrozen duckling if you can get it.

Heat oven to 400°.

Remove the neck, heart and liver from inside the duckling and set aside. Rinse the bird well under cold running water.

Drain and turn the duck upside down for a few minutes so all excess liquid runs out. Cut off the wing tips and reserve with the neck and giblets. Trim off excess skin and visible fat from the neck and body cavities.

Season the duck inside and out with salt and pepper. Place inside the duck: the liver, apple pieces, orange pieces, herbs, and onion.

Place a rack in the bottom of the roasting pan. If you do not have a rack, cover the bottom of the pan with apples cut in half, cut side down, and place the duck on top, breast side up. Roast for 45 minutes.

Reverse the position of the roasting pan (turn it from back to front) and cook for 45 more minutes. For a medium to medium-rare duck, the juice runs slightly pink when the thigh meat is pierced.

Even if you prefer duck well done, take it from the oven when medium rare, as it will cook more when you reheat it after making the sauce. The juice will be transparent when the duck is well done.

Remove duck from the oven and let cool. Using a sharp boning knife and starting at the neck, remove each breast half from the bone in one piece by scraping back carefully, making sure the knife's edge is held against the bone while you pull the meat away gently with your other hand.

Repeat with the other breast, then cut off the legs at the hip socket. Cover the carved meat and refrigerate. Save the carcass and all the trimmings for the stock.

After you have made your sauce and are ready to serve, preheat the broiler. Place the cut-up duck pieces on a baking pan and put under the broiler to reheat and to crisp the skin, for 3 to 4 minutes.

*(continued)*

# PRUNE AND MANGO SAUCE

*The prunes' dark color and the striking bright orange of the mangoes make this a beautiful sauce; it is one of my favorites. Remember, you can always substitute peaches for mangoes. The sauce also complements pork well.*

**MAKES 1½ CUPS**

*1 cup port wine*
*2 dozen pitted prunes*
*1 teaspoon unsalted butter*
*2 shallots, peeled and minced fine*
*¼ cup sherry wine vinegar*
*¼ cup honey*

*1 tablespoon green peppercorns in*
  *water, drained*
*2 cups Duck Stock (page 235)*
*½ teaspoon minced fresh ginger*
*1 cup mango cubes, about ¼ inch*

In a heavy, nonreactive saucepan, bring the port wine to a boil, then turn off heat and add the prunes. Let rest for about 30 minutes until the prunes have plumped. In a sauté pan, heat the butter over medium heat until light brown, then add the shallots and cook until they are translucent, not brown.

Add the vinegar and let bubble until reduced by half. Add the honey, green peppercorns, the wine from the prunes (but not the prunes), the stock, and the ginger. Let bubble until 1½ cups remain. Strain through a fine sieve into a clean saucepan. Add the mango and prunes.

Cook for 2 to 3 minutes and serve with the duckling.

# Black Cherry, Pearl Onion, and Kirsch Sauce

*This delicious sauce is a classic recipe. The sugar and vinegar reduction at the beginning of the preparation is an important process that brings balance and personality to the sauce.*

**MAKES 1 ½ CUPS**

⅓ cup sugar
⅔ cup red wine vinegar
24 pearl onions, packaged in
   water; not cocktail onions in
   vinegar
2 cups port wine
24 pitted black sweet cherries,
   canned in heavy syrup

1 cup fresh orange juice
2 tablespoons Kirsch liqueur,
   optional
2 sprigs fresh thyme
¼ teaspoon ground cinnamon
2 cups Duck Stock (page 235)
Salt and pepper to taste

In a stainless steel saucepan with a heavy bottom, cook the sugar and vinegar together over medium heat until the liquid has reduced to ¼ cup. Add the onions and cook a few minutes until they caramelize (become lightly browned and glazed). Add the port wine, bring to a boil, then reduce heat slightly and let bubble briskly until the volume is reduced by half.

Now, add the cherries with their juice, the orange juice, Kirsch, if using, thyme, cinnamon, and stock. Let bubble over low heat until 1½ cups of sauce remain. Adjust seasoning with salt and pepper and serve.

# Honey-Glazed Roast Duck

*In this recipe, the duck meat is moist and tender and the glaze turns a beautiful dark brown mahogany color. It is an easy dish to make and foolproof. If your duck is frozen, thaw it slowly in the refrigerator for at least 24 hours; 48 hours is even better. A fresh duckling would be great if you can find it. Serve the duck with basmati rice.*

**MAKES 2 SERVINGS**

### DUCK
1 4½- to 5-pound duck
Salt and freshly ground black
    pepper to taste
8 whole cloves
1 orange
2 sprigs fresh thyme

### HONEY GLAZE
2 cups orange juice (or papaya,
    mango, or pineapple juice)
¼ cup apple cider vinegar
3 tablespoons vanilla extract
1 tablespoon soy sauce
¼ teaspoon ground cloves
¼ teaspoon ground cinnamon

1 sprig rosemary, chopped fine
1 tablespoon chopped fresh thyme
    leaves
¼ cup honey

### SAUCE
Neck, wings, and giblets of the
    duck
2 sprigs fresh thyme
1 onion, peeled and chopped
1 carrot, peeled and chopped
1 tablespoon sunflower oil
2 cups water
2 tablespoons unsalted butter
Salt and pepper

*Make the duck:* Heat oven to 400°.

Remove the neck, heart, and liver from inside the duckling and rinse the bird well under cold running water. Drain and turn the duck upside down for a few minutes so all excess liquids run out.

Cut off the wing tips and reserve with the neck and giblets (see Duck Stock, page 235). Trim off excess skin and visible fat from the neck and body cavities.

Season the duck inside and out with salt and pepper. Stick the cloves in the orange, then cut the orange into quarters. Stuff the bird with the orange sections, the sprigs of thyme, and the duck liver.

Place a rack in the bottom of the roasting pan. If you do not have a rack, cover the bottom of the pan with oranges cut in half, cut side down, and place the duck on top, breast side up. Roast for 45 minutes.

*Make the glaze:* While the duck is roasting, mix all ingredients in a medium sauccpan. Bring to a boil, then reduce heat to medium high and let cook until about 1½ cups remain, about 25 minutes.

Strain the glaze through a fine sievc. Set aside ½ cup for the sauce.

*Finish the duck:* Reverse the position of the roasting pan (turn it from back to front), brush with the glaze, using a paintbrush. Make sure the bird is well covered. Take out the duckling every 15 minutes to brush on more glaze.

*Make the sauce:* In a saucepan, combine the duck parts, thyme, onion, carrot, and oil. Sauté for a few minutes until the onion starts to brown. Add the water and reduce over medium heat until ½ cup of liquid remains. Strain through a fine sieve and add to the reserved glaze. Add butter and salt and pepper to taste.

Cook duck for 45 more minutes until skin is a dark mahogany brown and crisp. For a medium to medium-rare duck, the juice runs slightly pink when the thigh meat is pierced. Remove the roast duck from the oven and let cool.

Using a sharp boning knife and starting at the neck, remove each breast half from the bone in one piece by scraping back carefully, making sure the knife's edge is held against the bone while you pull the meat away gently with your other hand. Repeat with the other breast, then cut off the legs at the hip socket. Serve with the sauce.

# *Turkey Breast*

## WITH WILD MUSHROOMS

*In this dish wild mushrooms add a little glamour to plain old turkey. Well suited for a family dinner or a spur-of-the-moment dinner party. If you can't find the mushrooms specified in the recipe, just use what is available.*

**MAKES 4 SERVINGS**

4 turkey breast steaks (about 8 to 10 ounces each), ¼ to ½ inch thick
Salt and freshly ground black pepper to taste
All-purpose flour for dredging
1 tablespoon olive oil
3 tablespoons unsalted butter, divided

1 tablespoon minced shallots
2 tablespoons minced garlic
4 ounces oyster mushrooms
4 ounces cremini mushrooms
4 ounces shiitake mushrooms
½ cup peeled, seeded, and chopped tomatoes
½ cup Chicken Stock (page 233)

Season turkey steaks with salt and pepper, and dredge lightly in flour; dust off any excess. In a large, nonstick sauté pan, heat the olive oil and 1 tablespoon of the butter until light brown. Add the turkey and sauté for 3 to 4 minutes on each side, or until cooked. Set aside and keep warm.

Add the shallots to the same sauté pan and cook for 2 minutes. Add the garlic and cook for 1 minute until fragrant. Add the mushrooms and sauté for 2 minutes.

Add the tomatoes and cook another 2 minutes. Add the stock and stir to scrape up any browned bits on the pan bottom. Stir in the remaining butter, if desired.

Serve the mushroom sauce on top of the turkey steaks.

# Meats

### Herb-Crusted Rack of Lamb

### Grilled Lamb Chops with Sunflower Seeds and Cumin Vinaigrette

### Roasted Pork Loin with Aromatic Vegetables

### Pork Tenderloin with Three-Peppercorn Sauce

### Jerked Pork Chops

### Roasted Pork Chops with Caramelized Onions

### Grilled Pork Chops on Onion and Bell Pepper Relish

### Orange-Glazed Pork Tenderloin

### Daube Provençale

### Roasted Filet Mignon with Shallot, Pinot Noir, and Pistachio Sauce

### Roasted New York Steak with Calamata Olive Tapenade

### Grilled Steak Chimichurri

### Roasted Veal Chops with Green Peppercorn Sauce

### Roasted Veal Loin with Shiitake Mushrooms

### Pan-Seared Veal Chops with Lime and Scallions

### Osso Buco Provençale

### Veal Loin with Roasted Shallots and Peas

# Herb-Crusted Rack of Lamb

*The Left Bank has offered this dish as a special-of-the-day for seventeen years, and every time, it's a sellout by 9:00 P.M. The sweetness of the roasted garlic makes a good companion for the lamb. Serve Parisienne Potatoes (page 192) alongside.*

**MAKES 2 SERVINGS**

1 rack of lamb with 8 to 9 chops
   (18 to 22 ounces)
Salt and freshly ground black
   pepper to taste
1 tablespoon chopped fresh
   cilantro leaves
1 teaspoon grated orange zest
1 sprig fresh thyme

1 sprig fresh oregano
2 garlic cloves
¼ cup fresh bread crumbs
1 tablespoon Dijon mustard
1 teaspoon mustard seeds
¼ cup port wine
½ cup Brown Beef Stock
   (page 236)

Heat oven to 350°.

Sprinkle lamb with salt and pepper. Heat a medium frying pan over high heat, then sear the lamb on each side for a few minutes. Do not add any fat to the pan.

Cover exposed bone tips with aluminum foil, then place the lamb in a roasting pan and cook 7 to 10 minutes.

Meanwhile, mix cilantro, orange zest, thyme, oregano, garlic and bread crumbs in a food processor, and pulse to blend. Remove the lamb from the oven. Coat the rounded outside layer of the meat with mustard, and press the bread-crumb mixture lightly over the top. Place lamb under the broiler for a couple of minutes to brown the bread mixture. Remove the rack of lamb to a warmed platter and set aside in a warm place.

*(continued)*

Add the mustard seeds, port wine, and stock to the roasting pan, and bring to a boil on the stovetop. Let the glaze boil and reduce for 2 to 3 minutes.

Carve the rack of lamb to separate the chops. Spoon 2 tablespoons of the glaze on the bottom of each dinner plate, arrange the chops on the plate, and serve with Roasted Rosemary Garlic (page 190) and Parisienne Potatoes.

# Grilled Lamb Chops
## WITH SUNFLOWER SEEDS AND CUMIN VINAIGRETTE

*This is one of my favorite outdoor recipes. Lamb chops cooked on the grill take on a wonderful, smoky flavor that's a perfect counterpoint to their rich taste. The Sunflower and Cumin Vinaigrette adds a tangy note.*

*Use sunflower seeds that have been hulled and are not heavily salted; they are sometimes available at natural foods stores. You can make this recipe with other nuts, such as toasted, chopped pecans. The vinaigrette is also excellent as a dressing for a green salad topped with sliced, grilled chicken breasts.*

**MAKES 4 SERVINGS**

*8 lamb loin chops, 1 to 1½ inches thick*

**MARINADE**
*2 large sprigs fresh rosemary*
*4 garlic cloves, peeled*
*¾ cup olive oil*
*¼ cup red wine vinegar*

**SUNFLOWER SEEDS AND CUMIN VINAIGRETTE**
*1 tablespoon whole cumin seeds*
*4 tablespoons sherry vinegar*
*2 tablespoons sunflower seeds*
*1 cup peeled, seeded, and chopped tomatoes*
*1 teaspoon fresh thyme leaves*
*½ cup extra-virgin olive oil*
*2 tablespoons hot water*
*¼ teaspoon salt*
*¼ teaspoon pepper*

*Marinate the lamb:* In boiling water, blanch the rosemary sprigs for 10 seconds (this helps release their flavor).

Remove and drain. Combine garlic, oil, and vinegar, and add the rosemary.

In a shallow glass baking dish, arrange the lamb chops side by side. Pour the marinade over the chops. Cover and refrigerate overnight.

*Make the vinaigrette:* Combine the cumin seeds and vinegar in a small saucepan and heat to boiling. This will bring out the flavor of the cumin. Let cook until only 1 tablespoon of vinegar remains. Pour into a blender.

Add the sunflower seeds, tomatoes, and thyme, then blend for 1 minute.

With the motor running, slowly pour in the olive oil, then the hot water and salt and pepper. The vinaigrette will keep, covered, in the refrigerator, for a few days. Bring to room temperature and shake well before using.

*Grill the lamb:* Prepare the grill for medium to high heat.

Grill the chops for 3 to 4 minutes on each side until medium rare or to your liking. To serve, ladle a little of the vinaigrette onto the bottom of each dinner plate, and top with 2 chops per person.

# Roasted Pork Loin

## WITH AROMATIC VEGETABLES

*M*y mother would prepare this dish on Sunday afternoons. She made enough to feed 14 people, even if we had only 7 for dinner. Cut all the vegetables the same size, to cook evenly and look attractive. After you have prepared this dish a few times, I'm sure it will become one of your favorites. It has so much finesse.

**MAKES 4 SERVINGS**

### ROAST
1 2½-pound boneless pork loin
    roast
6 garlic cloves, peeled
1 tablespoon freshly ground black
    pepper

### MARINADE
1 cup olive oil
½ cup pineapple juice
¼ cup apple cider vinegar
4 garlic cloves, peeled
2 sprigs fresh rosemary
1 bay leaf

2 tablespoons olive oil, divided
20 baby onions or pearl onions,
    peeled
10 very small, round potatoes
    (maximum 2 inches in
    diameter), peeled
2 large carrots, peeled and cut
    diagonally into ½-inch slices
3 cups Brown Beef Stock
    (page 236), divided
1 cup port wine
3 sprigs fresh thyme

*Marinate the roast:* Use a small, sharp knife to cut 6 slits in the pork roast. Make the slits about 1½ to 2 inches deep. Insert the whole cloves of garlic in the cuts. Sprinkle the roast with pepper and place it in a glass dish.

Combine the marinade ingredients and pour over the pork roast. Cover and refrigerate overnight.

*Cook the roast:* The next day, heat the oven to 350°.

Place a roasting pan on the stovetop (you may have to use 2 burners) and heat 1 tablespoon of the olive oil over medium-high heat.

Remove the pork roast from the marinade and pat it dry. Brown the roast in the hot oil on all sides until golden brown. Place the roasting pan in the oven and bake the pork for about 45 minutes, or until a meat thermometer reads 150°.

*Prepare the vegetables:* While the roast is cooking, heat the other tablespoon of olive oil in a large saucepan over medium heat. Add the onions and potatoes, and sauté until golden brown. Add the carrots and stir a minute, then add 2 cups of the stock. Reduce the heat so that the mixture bubbles gently, and cook until the vegetables are tender.

When the pork roast is done, remove the pan from the oven, then take the roast from the pan and place it on a serving platter. Cover the meat with aluminum foil and keep it warm.

*To finish:* Place the roasting pan on the stove, pour in the remaining cup of stock and the port. Add the fresh thyme. Stir and scrape over high heat, then lower the heat and let bubble until only 1 cup of liquid remains in the roasting pan.

Strain the liquid through a fine sieve and add to the vegetables. If the roast is tied with string, remove and discard the string. Carve the roast into ½-inch thick slices. Place the sliced pork roast on a serving platter and surround with the vegetables. Serve the sauce on the side.

# Pork Tenderloin

## WITH THREE-PEPPERCORN SAUCE

*I* love black peppercorns, especially with tender roast pork. I have made hundreds of sauces over the years but none that was as rich, creamy, spicy, and smooth as this one. You can also serve the peppercorn sauce with beef tenderloin, New York strip steak, or duck breast.

**MAKES 4 SERVINGS**

2 pork tenderloins, approximately
   2 pounds total
Salt and freshly ground black
   pepper to taste
1 tablespoon sunflower oil

**MARINADE**
1 cup extra-virgin olive oil
⅓ cup red wine vinegar
2 bay leaves
10 whole black peppercorns
2 sprigs fresh thyme
3 sprigs fresh rosemary
½ onion, peeled and cut into
1- inch cubes

**THREE-PEPPERCORN SAUCE**
2 shallots, peeled and finely
   chopped
1 tablespoon red wine vinegar
¼ cup Cabernet Sauvignon or dry
   red wine
½ cup Brown Beef Stock
   (page 236)
¼ cup heavy whipping cream
1 teaspoon green peppercorns in
   water, drained
1 teaspoon freshly ground black
   pepper
1 teaspoon freshly ground white
   pepper
¼ teaspoon salt
2 tablespoons unsalted butter,
   optional

*Marinate the pork:* Place the pork tenderloins in the marinade overnight.

*Roast the pork:* Remove from marinade and salt and pepper each tenderloin to taste. In a roasting pan, heat the sunflower oil and when hot, sauté tenderloins over medium heat for 2 minutes on each side. Roast in preheated 400° oven for 7 to 8 minutes.

*Make the sauce:* Remove the pork from the roasting pan and set aside. Remove the excess fat from the pan, add the shallots and cook for 1 minute. Add the vinegar and wine, and boil gently until reduced by one third. Add the stock and cream. Bring the mixture to a boil, add the peppercorns, black and white peppers, salt, and optional butter. Remove from the heat and swirl the pan to melt the butter. Slice the pork on the diagonal and serve on top of the sauce.

# Jerked Pork Chops

*The first time I tasted this dish was in a small Cuban restaurant in Miami. It took me a long time to duplicate the spicy taste of the seasoning, but you'll agree that the flavor is out of this world. Use this seasoning for chicken and fish as well.*

**MAKES 4 SERVINGS**

**JERK SEASONING**
2 tablespoons chopped onion
2 teaspoons chopped fresh thyme
   leaves
½ teaspoon freshly ground nutmeg
1 teaspoon ground cinnamon
½ cup chopped scallions
1 Scotch Bonnet pepper

2 tablespoons Worcestershire
   sauce
1 teaspoon ground allspice
1 tablespoon red wine vinegar
2 tablespoons vegetable oil
1 tablespoon soy sauce

8 1-inch thick pork chops

Blend all seasoning ingredients in a food processor until finely chopped. Place the pork chops side by side in a glass dish. Cover with the Jerk Seasoning. Cover the dish and refrigerate at least 2 hours.

Preheat the grill to medium heat. Grill the chops 5 to 7 minutes on each side, or to your liking.

# Roasted Pork Chops
## WITH CARAMELIZED ONIONS

*If you are an onion lover, you'll probably use this recipe with veal chops, chicken breasts, or even fish. The onions and Gorgonzola cheese combine to make an exceptional, rich taste. (You can substitute a mild goat cheese or blue cheese for the Gorgonzola, if desired.) Make the caramelized onions up to 2 days ahead, cover them, and refrigerate.*

**MAKES 4 SERVINGS**

### CARAMELIZED ONIONS
1 tablespoon unsalted butter
1 tablespoon peanut oil
1½ pounds red onions, peeled and
    sliced
1 tablespoon sugar
¼ cup red wine vinegar
½ cup Chicken Stock (page 233)

### SAUCE
3 tablespoons unsalted butter,
    divided
2 shallots, peeled and finely
    chopped
½ cup finely chopped red onion
1 cup red Zinfandel or dry red
    wine
2 sprigs fresh rosemary
1 cup Brown Beef Stock
    (page 236)

### PORK CHOPS
4 bone-in pork loin chops, 1 inch
    thick
⅓ cup finely crumbled mild
    Gorgonzola cheese
4 sprigs fresh rosemary

*Make the onions:* Heat the butter and oil in a large sauté pan, then add the onions, stir, and cook until golden brown. Be careful not to burn the onions. Add the sugar, vinegar, and stock, and cook over *very low heat* until all liquid has evaporated. Remove from heat.

*Make the sauce:* In a stainless steel saucepan, heat 1 tablespoon of the butter over medium-high heat and sauté the shallots and red onion until translucent, not brown. Add the Zinfandel and let boil gently until volume is reduced by half. Add the rosemary and stock, and cook until reduced by half again. Strain through a fine sieve. Remove from heat and stir in remaining butter, 1 tablespoon at a time. Hold sauce in a warm place until needed.

*Make the chops:* Heat oven to 350°. Trim the chops very well of fat and place the trimmings in a heavy, ovenproof skillet or roasting pan.

Heat the skillet and sauté the pork trimmings without any additional oil until they render enough fat to cover the bottom of the skillet. Remove the pork pieces.

Add the chops and sauté on one side for 3 to 4 minutes. Turn the chops over and remove from the heat. Arrange the caramelized onions evenly on each chop. Divide the Gorgonzola cheese and crumble it on each pork chop. Place 1 sprig of rosemary on each chop.

Place the skillet in the oven and cook for 5 to 7 more minutes. Serve with the sauce.

# Grilled Pork Chops

## ON ONION AND BELL PEPPER RELISH

*P*ork chops do not have to be dry and overcooked. In this recipe, the grilled pork chops are juicy and smoky; served with the bell pepper confit, they're hard to beat. Just don't cook them too long. At The Left Bank restaurant, we reserve this delicate relish for a fillet of red snapper that is baked very slowly in the oven. One day I tried it at home with grilled pork chops, and it was fantastic. You'll love its tangy flavor.

**MAKES 4 SERVINGS**

4 8-ounce bone-in pork loin chops,
    about 1 to 1½ inches thick,
    well trimmed
Salt and freshly ground black
    pepper to taste

**MARINADE**
1 cup extra-virgin olive oil
⅓ cup red wine vinegar
2 bay leaves
10 whole black peppercorns
2 sprigs fresh thyme
3 sprigs fresh rosemary
½ onion, peeled and cut into
    1-inch cubes

**ONION AND BELL PEPPER RELISH**
2 pounds sweet Spanish onions,
    peeled and thinly sliced
1 red bell pepper, seeded and cut
    into matchstick-size strips
1 green bell pepper, seeded and
    cut into matchstick-size strips
1 tablespoon walnut oil
1 teaspoon balsamic vinegar
2 tablespoons light brown sugar
¼ cup port wine

*Marinate the pork:* Combine the marinade ingredients and stir to blend. Place pork chops in the marinade (in a glass, ceramic or stainless steel dish, or in a heavy-duty plastic zipper-lock bag) and refrigerate overnight.

*Make the relish:* In a stainless steel pan, sauté the onions and bell peppers in the oil until onions are translucent (do not burn them). Add the vinegar, sugar, and port wine, and cook at a very low heat until liquid evaporates. Onions and peppers should still be a little firm to the bite but sweet and caramelized.

*Cook the pork:* To cook, prepare the grill for medium heat grilling. Grill the chops for 4 to 5 minutes on each side, or until cooked to your liking. Salt and pepper to taste. Serve on a bed of Onion and Bell Pepper Relish.

# Orange-Glazed Pork Tenderloin

*When pork tenderloin is cooked properly, it is as moist, tender, and flavorful as veal. The secret is to undercook it slightly. Do not be afraid to eat pork slightly rosy, as pork is safe to eat rare. Instead of flattening the pork, you can cut it into ¾-inch-thick medallions and cook it a minute or two longer. Great with couscous, wild rice, basmati rice, or buttered noodles.*

**MAKES 4 SERVINGS**

2 pork tenderloins, about 2 pounds total
1 tablespoon unsalted butter
1 tablespoon olive oil
2 shallots, peeled and finely chopped
¼ cup red wine vinegar
¼ cup Cabernet Sauvignon or dry red wine
1 tablespoon honey
2 tablespoons frozen orange juice concentrate, thawed
½ cup heavy whipping cream
Salt and freshly ground black pepper to taste
Thin strips of orange zest, for garnish, optional (see Note)

Cut the meat crosswise into pieces 2 inches thick, then use a meat mallet or pounder to flatten them to ¼ inch thick. (Or cut them crosswise into ¾-inch thick medallions.) Salt and pepper the pork pieces.

Heat the butter and olive oil in a large sauté pan, then sauté the pork over medium heat for 2 minutes on each side. You may need to do this in batches. Remove the sautéed pork from the skillet to a plate and keep warm while you make the sauce.

Pour any excess fat from the skillet, then add the shallots and cook for 1 minute. Add the vinegar and wine, and let cook until volume is reduced by one third. Add the honey, orange juice concentrate, and cream. Bring the mixture to a boil, add salt and pepper to adjust seasoning, and serve over the pork. Sprinkle the serving platter with orange zest, if desired.

**NOTE:** A zester is a kitchen tool that lets you shave tiny, shallow strips of peel (or zest) from oranges and other citrus fruits. Look for one that has four small holes instead of one large one. Zesters are widely available in kitchen supply stores and in the housewares sections of department stores.

# Daube Provençale

*A hearty beef stew may not sound like Sunshine Cuisine, but it's a classic in the sunny south of France where I grew up. My mother used to make a daube provençale at least twice a month, and you probably will, too! I love this dish served with small Parisienne Potatoes (page 192) around the plate.*

**MAKES 4 SERVINGS**

6 bacon strips, cut into 1-inch
  pieces
2 pounds boneless chuck roast or
  top round, well-trimmed and
  cut into 2-inch cubes
20 pearl onions (see Note)
20 baby carrots, about 1½ inches
  long
1 tablespoon minced fresh garlic
1 cup white wine
2 cups peeled, seeded, and
  chopped tomatoes

4 tablespoons tomato paste
1 teaspoon minced fresh thyme
  leaves
1 teaspoon minced fresh rosemary
  leaves
1 bay leaf
1 cup Brown Beef Stock
  (page 236)
¼ teaspoon salt
½ teaspoon freshly ground black
  pepper

In a large skillet or Dutch oven, cook the bacon over medium heat until crisp and light brown. Remove the bacon from the skillet and reserve, leaving the fat in the skillet.

Add some of the beef cubes to the skillet and brown well on all sides. Add as many meat cubes as you can without crowding, so meat will brown properly. Remove each batch of browned beef from the skillet and set aside. You may need to add a little olive oil.

*(continued)*

When all the beef has been browned and removed, add the pearl onions to the remaining fat in the skillet and cook, stirring occasionally, until they are golden brown. Add the carrots and garlic, and stir.

When the garlic is fragrant, about 1 minute, add the browned beef cubes plus any juices they have given off, the reserved bacon, wine, tomatoes, tomato paste, thyme, rosemary, bay leaf, and stock.

Reduce the heat to low, cover, and let simmer for 1½ to 2 hours, stirring occasionally, until the meat is very tender. After about an hour, check to see how liquid the stew seems; for a thicker stew, set the lid slightly ajar and continue cooking.

Adjust the salt and pepper, and remove the bay leaf.

Serve with Parisienne Potatoes arranged around the plate.

**NOTE:** If you can't find pearl onions in the produce department, use the kind packed in water. Do not use pickled onions!

# Roasted Filet Mignon

## WITH SHALLOT, PINOT NOIR, AND PISTACHIO SAUCE

*The Shallot, Pinot Noir, and Pistachio Sauce tastes wonderful and is so easy to make. You can grill the steaks instead of roasting them, but don't skip the sauce! Start the sauce first, so it will be ready when the steaks are roasted.*

**MAKES 4 SERVINGS**

### STEAKS
4 beef filet mignon steaks, 6 to 8
    ounces each
1 teaspoon unsalted butter
1 teaspoon olive oil
Salt and freshly ground black
    pepper to taste

### SAUCE
3 tablespoons unsalted butter,
    divided
1 tablespoon olive oil

4 shallots, separated if double and
    sliced into thin rings
2 cups Pinot Noir
2 cups Brown Beef Stock
    (page 236)
½ cup chopped, unsalted
    pistachio nuts
1 teaspoon minced fresh parsley
Salt and freshly ground black
    pepper to taste

Remove steaks from refrigerator and heat the oven to 375°.

*Start the sauce:* In a sauté pan, heat 1 tablespoon of the butter with the olive oil over medium heat until very hot. Add the shallots, lower the heat, and cook slowly until they begin to soften. When the shallots are translucent, not brown, add the wine and let boil gently until volume is reduced to approximately ¾ cup. Add the stock and the nuts, and continue to cook until ¾ cup is left. Remove from the heat and swirl in the remaining 2 tablespoons of butter and the parsley. Adjust seasoning with salt and pepper.

*Roast the steaks:* In an ovenproof roasting pan on the stove, heat the butter and oil until sizzling, then cook the steaks on all sides until they are a nice golden brown. Set the roasting pan in the oven and roast for 5 to 7 minutes.

*To serve:* Pour 2 tablespoons of sauce on the bottom of the dinner plate and place the filet mignon in the middle. Serve with Parisienne Potatoes (page 192) and fresh green beans.

# Roasted New York Steak

## WITH CALAMATA OLIVE TAPENADE

*Oven roasting produces flavorful, juicy results, and it is easy to do for 1 or 2 portions at a time. You can grill the steaks, if you prefer. Once you've turned the steaks, spread the cooked sides with tapenade, then cover the grill with a lid and finish cooking. The tapenade is delicious spread on toasted bread or tossed with pasta. It keeps in the refrigerator for several days.*

**MAKES 4 SERVINGS**

**STEAKS**
4 boneless New York strip steaks,
    8 to 10 ounces each
1 tablespoon olive oil
1 teaspoon unsalted butter

**CALAMATA OLIVE TAPENADE**
1 cup pitted black Calamata
    olives
2 garlic cloves, peeled

1 tablespoon capers, well drained
2 anchovies, drained
1 teaspoon Dijon mustard
¼ cup extra-virgin olive oil
Juice of ½ lemon
1 tablespoon Armagnac liqueur,
    optional
½ teaspoon freshly ground black
    pepper

Preheat oven to 425°.

*Make the tapenade:* Combine all ingredients in a food processor fitted with a steel blade. Process until puréed into a thick paste. If needed, add a little more olive oil, 1 tablespoon at a time. The recipe needs no additional salt because of the anchovies and olives.

*Roast the steaks:* In a roasting pan over 2 burners on the stove, heat the oil and butter. When sizzling and golden brown, place the steaks in the pan and cook for 2 minutes. Turn the steaks on their sides and brown on sides for 2 minutes.

Turn the steaks so the uncooked sides are down; smooth 1 tablespoon of tapenade evenly on top of each steak, then place the roasting pan in the oven and cook for 6 to 10 minutes, or to desired doneness.

Serve with Garlic and Onion-Roasted Potatoes (page 191).

# Grilled Steak Chimichurri

*Chimichurri is the South American version of pesto and is available in most Latin food markets already prepared. You can marinate the steaks for a couple of hours before grilling them or serve the Chimichurri on the side as a condiment.*

**MAKES 4 SERVINGS**

**CHIMICHURRI**
*1 bunch parsley leaves, stems discarded, well washed*
*3 garlic cloves*
*½ cup extra-virgin olive oil*
*1 tablespoon balsamic vinegar*
*1 tablespoon red wine vinegar*

*1 small Scotch Bonnet pepper*
*Salt and freshly ground black pepper to taste*

*4 12-ounce New York strip steaks, approximately 1 inch thick*

In a food processor, mix all Chimichurri ingredients until chopped fine. If you are going to marinate the steak, add an extra ½ cup of olive oil. Pour over steaks, cover, and refrigerate overnight.

Heat the grill to high. Let steak warm to room temperature. Cook on an open grill for 5 to 6 minutes on each side for a nice medium rare.

VEAL

# Roasted Veal Chops

## WITH GREEN PEPPERCORN SAUCE

*I love to use Armagnac in my sauces, but brandy is just as good. While the veal is roasting, make the rich, smooth sauce. Be careful of the roasting pan; as it gets very hot.*

**MAKES 2 SERVINGS**

**VEAL**
2 10- to 12-ounce veal rib or
 loin chops
1 teaspoon unsalted butter
1 teaspoon olive oil

**PEPPERCORN SAUCE**
1 tablespoon unsalted butter
1 shallot, finely chopped
2 tablespoons Armagnac or
 brandy

2 tablespoons frozen orange juice
 concentrate, thawed
¼ cup Brown Beef Stock
 (page 236)
1 teaspoon green peppercorns in
 water, drained
¼ cup heavy whipping cream
2 tablespoons unsalted butter,
 optional

*Make the veal:* Preheat oven to 400°. Lightly pound the chops to flatten them slightly to a maximum thickness of 1 inch.

In an ovenproof roasting pan on top of the stove, heat the butter and oil over medium heat. When sizzling, sear the chops on one side for 3 to 4 minutes. Remove the pan from the stove, turn the chops over, and roast in the oven for 10 minutes. (Meanwhile start the sauce.) Turn the chops again and cook for another 2 minutes, or until the veal is done to your liking. The meat should be pink in the center.

*Make the sauce:* Place 1 tablespoon butter and chopped shallot in a sauté pan, and cook over medium heat until lightly brown (do not burn them). Add the Armagnac and flambé to burn off the alcohol. (Light the end of a wooden kitchen skewer, then touch the flame to the pan; it will blaze for a few minutes, then subside.)

Add the orange juice concentrate and the stock, and let bubble until volume is reduced by half. Add the green peppercorns and cream, and let cook until thick enough to coat the back of a spoon. For a smooth and rich sauce, if desired, swirl in the additional butter off the heat just before serving.

# Roasted Veal Loin

## WITH SHIITAKE MUSHROOMS

*A*sk *your butcher or supermarket meat manager to special-order veal tenderloin, a tender, flavorful cut worth going out of your way to find. Ask for "veal butt tenders." Pork tenderloin works well, too.*

**MAKES 4 SERVINGS**

**VEAL**
4 veal loins, 5 to 6 ounces each
1 teaspoon unsalted butter
1 teaspoon olive oil

**MUSHROOMS**
4 tablespoons unsalted butter, divided
1 tablespoon olive oil
2 shallots, chopped
1 tablespoon balsamic vinegar
½ pound shiitake, oyster, or cremini mushrooms, sliced
½ cup port wine
1 cup Brown Beef Stock (page 236)
1 tablespoon green peppercorns, drained
Salt and freshly ground black pepper

*Make the veal:* Heat the oven to 375°. In an ovenproof roasting pan on the stove top, heat the butter and oil, and brown the loins on all sides until a nice golden brown. Roast about 15 minutes, or until an instant-read meat thermometer registers about 145° or rare.

*Make the mushrooms:* In a saucepan, heat 1 tablespoon butter with the olive oil. When hot, add the shallots and cook slowly until they begin to soften. When lightly browned, add the vinegar and let reduce for 2 minutes. Add the mushrooms and sauté rapidly. Add the port wine, stock, and green peppercorns, and boil gently until reduced by half. Remove from the heat, then stir in the remaining 3 tablespoons of butter. Add salt and pepper to taste.

*To serve:* Slice each veal loin crosswise into thin, ¼-inch slices. Pour a little sauce in the center of 4 warmed dinner plates, then arrange the veal on the plates. Serve with Parisienne Potatoes (page 192), or Garlic and Onion-Roasted Potatoes (page 191), and steamed fresh baby green beans.

# Pan-Seared Veal Chops

## WITH LIME AND SCALLIONS

*Lime juice adds a spark to these simple pan-sautéed veal chops. An easy but impressive entrée for a casual dinner with good friends.*

**MAKES 4 SERVINGS**

*1 tablespoon olive oil*
*3 tablespoons unsalted butter, divided*
*4 veal rib chops (with bone), 10 to 12 ounces each, 1 inch thick*
*4 scallions, cut into ¼-inch diagonal slices*
*1 leek, cut into ¼-inch diagonal slices*

*4 tablespoons fresh lime juice (see* Note)
*Zest of 1 lime, cut into very thin strips*
*¼ cup Chardonnay or dry white wine*
*¾ cup Brown Beef Stock (page 236)*

In a large sauté pan on top of the stove, heat the olive oil and 1 tablespoon of the butter. When the butter is hazelnut in color, reduce the heat to medium. Add the veal chops and sear until golden brown on both sides, turning once, about 10 minutes.

Add the scallions, leek, lime juice, zest, wine, and stock. Reduce heat to low, cover, and cook for 10 more minutes, or until the chops are cooked. They should be pink in the center.

Remove the chops and scallions from the pan and hold in a warm place. Increase the heat and reduce the liquid until ½ cup remains. Stir in the remaining 2 tablespoons of butter.

Serve 1 veal chop per plate and top with the scallions and 2 tablespoons of sauce per chop.

**NOTE:** If the lime juice is too tart for your taste, add just a *touch* of sugar; ¼ teaspoon should do the trick. You will not taste the sugar, but it will take some of the tartness out of the lime juice.

# Osso Buco Provençale

*You'll need about 3 pounds of veal shanks for this recipe, but much of that weight is bone. For a more rustic presentation, do not strain the sauce but leave it chunky. For a more refined look, strain out the solids and finish with a little butter as directed in the recipe. Veal shanks are traditionally prepared as osso buco—the name refers to the hole in the bone—and served with risotto. This recipe updates a classic.*

**MAKES 4 SERVINGS**

4 veal shanks, as big as you can get them, cut 1½ inches thick

Salt and pepper

½ cup all-purpose flour for dredging

2 tablespoons olive oil, divided

3 tablespoons unsalted butter, divided

½ cup finely chopped onion

½ cup prosciutto, sliced ¼ inch thick, then cut into ¼-inch cubes

½ cup finely chopped celery

½ cup finely chopped carrots

½ cup white wine

½ cup port wine

2 cups Brown Beef Stock (page 236)

1 cup Chicken Stock (page 233)

1 cup peeled, seeded, and chopped tomatoes

¼ cup tomato paste

½ cup pitted Calamata olives

2 tablespoons chopped fresh sweet basil leaves

Heat oven to 400°.

Season the veal shanks with salt and pepper and dust with flour, brushing off excess. In a Dutch oven or a deep ovenproof pan with a cover, heat 1 tablespoon of the olive oil and 1 tablespoon of the butter. When hot, add the shanks and brown on both sides. Make sure the shanks fit comfortably in the pan without crowding.

While the shanks are browning, heat 1 tablespoon olive oil in a sauté pan. Add the onion and sauté until translucent, not brown, about 5 minutes. Add the prosciutto and sauté 5 more minutes. Add the celery and carrots. Sauté 5 minutes more and transfer vegetables to the pan with the veal shanks.

Add the white wine and the port to the pan with the veal and let reduce until only ¼ cup remains. Add the stocks, tomatoes, and tomato paste, and stir to combine. Cover the pan, transfer to the oven, and cook until the meat pulls away from the bone, 90 minutes to 2 hours. Remove the pan from the oven, then carefully lift out the shanks; set aside to keep warm.

Strain the sauce through a fine sieve into a saucepan. Add the black olives and basil, taste, and adjust salt and pepper. Bring to a boil, then lower the heat and let bubble until reduced to about 1½ cups. Add the remaining butter and serve.

# Veal Loin

## WITH ROASTED SHALLOTS AND PEAS

*L*ittle veal loins are delicious and tender when oven roasted. Whole shallots add a lot of flavor and sweetness when they are roasted, and the tiny green peas give a nice contrast in texture.

**MAKES 4 SERVINGS**

1 tablespoon unsalted butter
1 tablespoon olive oil
4 veal loins, 5 to 6 ounces each
12 small shallots, peeled and left
   whole

¼ cup pancetta, cut into cubes
½ cup Brown Beef Stock
   (page 236)
1 pound fresh or frozen baby peas

Heat oven to 375°.

In an ovenproof roasting pan on the stovetop, heat the butter and oil. Add the veal loins and cook until golden brown on all sides. Add the shallots.

Place pan in the oven and cook veal loins for 10 minutes. Remove pan from the oven, turn the loins and the shallots over on the other side. Add the pancetta. Return pan to the oven for 2 minutes. Add the stock and the peas, and cook for 5 more minutes.

Remove from the oven, slice each veal loin crosswise into thin ¼-inch slices. Arrange on dinner plates and serve the peas and shallots alongside the veal.

# Vegetables

GREEN BEANS WITH CALAMATA OLIVES AND
TOASTED PINE NUTS

TOMATO HALVES PROVENÇALE

GLAZED CARROTS

GRILLED CORN, BLACK BEANS, AND
TOMATO RELISH

GRILLED CORN CUSTARD

LENTIL STEW

WHITE BEAN RAGOUT

THREE-BEAN RELISH

ROASTED SHALLOT FLAN

RATATOUILLE PROVENÇALE

ROASTED ROSEMARY GARLIC

GARLIC AND ONION-ROASTED POTATOES

PARISIENNE POTATOES

# Green Beans with Calamata Olives and Toasted Pine Nuts

*P*lain *green beans have never tasted this good! The secret is the earthy flavor of Calamata olives, tamed with a little garlic and tomato.*

**MAKES 4 SERVINGS**

¼ cup pine nuts
1 pound green beans
1 teaspoon unsalted butter
1 teaspoon olive oil
¼ cup minced onion

1 tablespoon minced garlic
½ cup peeled, seeded, and
    chopped tomatoes
¼ cup Calamata olives, pitted
    and chopped

In a small, nonstick frying pan, toast the pine nuts until golden brown. Remove from heat and reserve.

Remove the tips and tails from the green beans and cut them into 1½-inch lengths. Bring a big pot of salted water to a boil and poach the beans until tender but still firm, about 7 minutes. Drain into a colander.

In a sauté pan, heat the butter and oil and add the beans. Sauté 1 minute, then add the onion and cook until translucent, not brown.

Add the garlic, tomatoes, and olives. Sauté for a couple of minutes.

Add the pine nuts and serve immediately.

# Tomato Halves Provençale

*M*y mother use to prepare these baked tomatoes as a classic, simple, and delicious side dish for grilled steak or chicken. The flavor and texture of the freshly baked tomatoes and garlic are outstanding.

**MAKES 4 SERVINGS**

4 slices French bread, crusts
   removed
1 tablespoon minced garlic
1 tablespoon minced shallots
1 tablespoon minced fresh parsley

2 large, ripe tomatoes, cut in half
   crosswise
Salt and freshly ground black
   pepper to taste

In the food processor, combine the bread, garlic, shallots, and parsley. Process until finely chopped. Gently squeeze tomato halves to remove seeds and excess water. Salt and pepper the tomatoes and place, cut side down, to drain on a paper towel.

Heat the oven to 350°.

Arrange the tomatoes, cut side up, in a baking pan. Divide the crumb mixture evenly and pat onto each tomato half. Bake for 15 to 20 minutes until the bread crumbs are golden brown and the tomatoes are hot all the way through.

For an interesting variation, sprinkle crumbled goat cheese or feta cheese on the tomatoes just before baking.

# Glazed Carrots

*Sweet and flavorful carrots get the royal treatment with honey and dill.
Serve them with a simple grilled chicken.*

**MAKES 4 SERVINGS**

*5–6 carrots, no bigger than 1 inch
    in diameter and 5 inches long
2 tablespoons unsalted butter
1 tablespoon minced shallots
¼ cup Chicken Stock (page 233)*

*1 tablespoon honey
2 teaspoons minced fresh dill
Salt and freshly ground black
    pepper to taste*

Peel the carrots, then slice them diagonally about ¼ inch thick.

In a large saucepan, heat the butter until foamy, then add the shallots.
When the shallots are translucent, add the carrots and stock. Reduce the
heat to low, cover, and cook slowly until carrots are tender, about 10
minutes. Add the honey, dill, salt, and pepper. Serve immediately.

# Grilled Corn, Black Beans, and Tomato Relish

*This flavorful relish adds lots of taste to grilled meats. You can use canned black beans and nobody will know the difference (unless you have some professional chefs as guests!). Make the grilled corn ahead of time, or poach the shucked corn in boiling water for a few minutes and proceed with the recipe.*

**MAKES ABOUT 4 CUPS**

### GRILLED CORN

3 whole ears yellow corn in the
    husks
2 teaspoons unsalted butter,
    softened

4 ounces dried black beans

### TOMATO RELISH

1 cup peeled, seeded, and chopped
    tomatoes
2 scallions, cut into very thin
    diagonal slices
¼ cup finely diced red onion
1 tablespoon red wine vinegar
3 tablespoons olive oil
Salt and freshly ground black
    pepper to taste

*Grill the corn:* Carefully and gently pull back the green corn husks and remove the silky fibers inside. Be careful not to break off the husks. Cut about ¾ inch from the tip of each ear. Soak the corn in a large bowl of cool water for 30 minutes.

Drain the corn and pat dry. Rub the softened butter on the corn kernels and fold the husks back in place. Grill over a medium charcoal or gas fire for 15 to 20 minutes, turning the ears at least 3 times.

Remove the corn from the grill and, using an oven mitt to protect your hand, peel back the husks and cut off the kernels to make 2 cups.

*Cook the beans:* Prepare the black beans following the directions on the package. Be careful not to overcook them, as they should be slightly firm. Refrigerate the beans after cooking. You will need 1 cup for this recipe.

*Prepare the relish:* Mix the grilled corn kernels, black beans, and Tomato Relish ingredients in a bowl and chill for at least 1 hour.

# Grilled Corn Custard

*The next time you grill, prepare some ears of corn, too, so that you can make these beautiful little custards. The roasted corn will keep a day or so, covered, in the refrigerator. The cooked custards will also keep a day or two in the refrigerator.*

**MAKES 8 SERVINGS**

3 whole ears yellow corn,
   husks on
2 teaspoons unsalted butter,
   softened
¾ cup milk
1 cup heavy whipping cream

3 large eggs
1 red jalapeño pepper (to make
   1 tablespoon minced)
Salt and white pepper to taste
1 tablespoon minced fresh cilantro
   leaves

Gently pull back the husks from the corn and remove the silky fibers inside. Do not break off the husks because they protect the corn as it grills. Cut any unformed kernels off the top of the corn, about 1 inch.

Soak the corn in a large bowl of cool water for 30 minutes. Drain and pat dry. Use your fingers to rub the softened butter on the corn, then fold the husks back into place.

Grill the corn over a medium fire for 15 to 20 minutes, turning at least 3 times. Remove the corn from the grill and hold with an oven mitt while you fold back the husks and cut the kernels off the cobs to make 1½ cups.

Heat oven to 400°.

Place the milk, half the corn kernels and the remaining ingredients, except the cilantro, in a blender and blend for 1 minute. Strain through a fine sieve, then return the mixture to the blender. Add the cilantro and blend briefly.

Butter eight 3-ounce ramekins or spray them with a nonstick spray. Divide the remaining whole corn kernels among the ramekins. Ladle the custard into the ramekins. Place the ramekins in a baking pan and place in the oven on the middle rack. Carefully pour in enough boiling water to reach ¾ of the way up the sides of the dishes. Cook for 35 minutes, or until the custards have puffed and begun to brown lightly.

When the custards are done, remove the pan from the oven and let the ramekins sit in the hot water for 15 minutes. Then remove the ramekins and let the custards cool for at least an hour. They will fall slightly, but don't worry.

To serve, place ramekins on a baking sheet, for ease of handling, and reheat in a 350° oven for about 5 minutes. Then unmold custards onto dinner plates. The custards can also be microwaved for 30 seconds.

# Lentil Stew

*In this beautiful earthy stew, flecks of purple onion and snips of green chives accent rich brown lentils. Lentils don't have to be soaked before cooking, which gives them great potential for a side dish. This stew is also excellent made without the ham.*

**MAKES 4 SERVINGS**

1 cup lentils
2 cups Chicken Stock (page 233)
1 tablespoon olive oil
1 medium red onion, peeled and
    finely chopped
2 garlic cloves, peeled and very
    finely chopped
¼ cup red wine vinegar

1 slice baked ham, ¼ inch thick,
    cut into small cubes, optional
1 tablespoon finely chopped fresh
    chives
2 tablespoons unsalted butter,
    optional
Salt and freshly ground black
    pepper

Rinse the lentils in a colander under cold running water, then put them into a large stainless steel pot with the stock.

Bring to a boil, then reduce the heat so that the lentils just simmer, and let cook about 30 minutes. Lentils should be firm to the bite but cooked.

In a saucepan, heat the olive oil. When hot, add the onion and cook until it is translucent, not brown. Add the garlic and cook until it is fragrant, about 1 minute.

Add the vinegar and let cook until volume is reduced by half.

Stir in the lentils, ham, if using, chives, and butter, if desired. Season to taste with salt and pepper. Hold over low heat until serving time.

# White Bean Ragout

*I* *don't know about you, but I'm addicted to beans. When I tasted the White Bean Ragout recipe for this book, I was on a diet where no fat was allowed. Well, diet or no diet, I couldn't stop eating them! Great Northern beans are small and white and cook into tender little mouthfuls. Their mild flavor accepts seasonings beautifully. This bean dish is wonderful served with grilled pork chops. It's also tasty made without ham and pancetta and using vegetable stock instead of chicken.*

**MAKES 4 SERVINGS**

12 ounces (about 2 cups) Great
    Northern beans
5 cups water
1 onion, peeled and quartered
    through the root end
2 celery stalks, cut into chunks
3 garlic cloves, peeled and left
    whole
1 bay leaf
1 pound ham hocks

1 teaspoon unsalted butter
2 shallots, peeled and finely
    minced
2 ounces (about ½ cup) pancetta,
    cut into ¼-inch cubes
2 garlic cloves, peeled and minced
1 tablespoon white wine vinegar
1 cup Chicken Stock (page 233)
    or Vegetable Stock (page 231)
Salt

Pick through the beans for any stones or foreign objects and rinse them well in cold water. Put in a bowl or saucepan and add cool water to come about 2 inches above the beans. Let stand overnight to soak.

The next day, pour off the soaking water and put the beans and 5 cups water into a large saucepan or soup pot and bring to a boil. Add the onion, celery, garlic, bay leaf, and ham hock.

Lower heat so that beans just simmer gently, cover partially, and cook until the beans are tender but not mushy, 1½ to 2 hours. Stir often to prevent scorching. Drain the beans in a colander and discard the other ingredients.

*(continued)*

In a sauté pan over low heat, heat the butter, then add the shallots and pancetta, and cook gently for 2 minutes. Do not brown.

Add the garlic and sauté another minute.

Add the vinegar and let reduce for 1 minute. Add the cup of stock and the beans, and stir well to combine. Add salt to taste. Hold over very low heat until ready to serve.

# Three-Bean Relish

*If you're concerned with aesthetics, consider soaking and cooking the black beans separately so they don't leach into the white ones and turn them gray. This relish gets its zing from horseradish; for a milder, more Mediterranean variation, omit the horseradish and add more chopped fresh basil. The ham hock adds flavor, but it's not essential, if you'd rather have a meatless version. Serve the relish at room temperature or, better yet, make it the day before, refrigerate, and serve chilled.*

**MAKES 2½ CUPS**

⅓ cup red kidney beans
  (see Note)
⅓ cup black beans (see Note)
⅓ cup Great Northern beans
  (see Note)
3 cups water
1 onion, peeled and halved
  through the root end
1 large ham hock
1 bay leaf
½ cup peeled, seeded, and
  chopped tomatoes

½ cup finely chopped red onion
1 tablespoon finely chopped fresh
  sweet basil leaves
2 cloves garlic, peeled and minced
¼ cup olive oil
2 tablespoons balsamic vinegar
2 tablespoons prepared
  horseradish
Salt and freshly ground black
  pepper to taste

Pick through the beans to remove any stones, then rinse the beans in cold water. Place in a bowl or pot and add enough cold water to cover them by about 2 inches. Let the beans soak overnight.

The next day, pour out the soaking water and put the plumped beans into a large saucepan with 3 cups water. Bring to a boil and spoon off any froth or scum, then add the onion, ham hock, and bay leaf. Reduce the heat so that the beans just simmer gently, cover partially, and cook until the beans are tender, about 1½ hours. Stir often to prevent scorching.

When the beans are tender but not mushy, drain them in a colander. Remove and discard the onion, ham hock, and bay leaf. Let the beans cool to room temperature, then transfer to a serving bowl. Stir in the tomatoes, red onion, basil, garlic, olive oil, vinegar, horseradish, and season with salt and pepper.

**NOTE:** Dried beans are delicious and easy to cook if you keep these tips in mind. The older the beans, the longer they take to cook. Dried beans can become tender in as little as 45 minutes, or take as long as 2½ hours.

All dried beans except lentils need a preliminary soak to soften their skins and rehydrate them before they are cooked. Either let the beans stand, for 8 hours or overnight, in cool water to cover by about 2 inches, or use the quick method: Bring the beans and water to a boil, cook 2 minutes, then remove them from the heat and let stand, covered, for 1 hour. (Beans are easier to digest if you pour off the soaking water and use fresh water to cook them.)

Do not add salt until the beans are almost tender. Salt added at the beginning of cooking prevents the skins from softening.

# Roasted Shallot Flan

*O*nce you've made these tiny, savory custards, you can experiment with other vegetables, for example, a wild mushroom flan. If your rosemary has a woody, hard stem, strip the leaves and just use them. If your plant has tender stems, use the whole sprig.

**MAKES 6 SERVINGS**

1 tablespoon olive oil
4 large shallots, peeled
1 sprig fresh rosemary
¾ cup milk

1 cup heavy whipping cream
3 large eggs
Salt and freshly ground black
    pepper to taste

Heat oven to 400°.

In a small baking pan, combine the olive oil, shallots, and rosemary. Cover with aluminum foil and roast for 20 minutes. Remove from oven.

Place the shallot mixture in a blender, add the milk and blend until very smooth. Add the remaining ingredients and blend again. Strain through a fine sieve.

Butter six 3-ounce ramekins, and ladle in the shallot custard. Place the ramekins in a baking pan on the middle rack of the oven. Pour enough boiling water into the pan to reach ¾ of the way up the sides of the ramekins.

Cook for 35 minutes, or until the custards start to puff slightly.

Remove the pan from the oven, but leave the ramekins in the water bath for 15 minutes. Then remove them from the water and let stand at least 1 hour.

To serve, place ramekins on a baking sheet, for ease of handling, and reheat in a 350° oven for about 5 minutes. Then unmold custards onto dinner plates. The custards can also be microwaved for 30 seconds.

# Ratatouille Provençale

*This colorful, savory mix of purple eggplant, red and green peppers, and black, tangy olives is worth the cutting and chopping. Wonderful with all kinds of fish, chicken, grilled meat, even in an omelet. Eaten cold, with a big spoon, it is delectable.*

**MAKES 6 SERVINGS**

2 tablespoons olive oil

1 small eggplant, cut into ¾-inch dice, about 1½ cups

½ red bell pepper, cored, seeded, and cut into ½-inch by 2-inch strips

½ green bell pepper, cored, seeded, and cut into ½-inch by 2-inch strips

1 medium red onion, peeled and chopped into 1-inch cubes, about 1 cup

2 medium zucchini, ends trimmed, cut lengthwise into quarters, then into 1-inch chunks

2 medium yellow squash, ends trimmed, cut lengthwise into quarters, then into 1-inch chunks

½ cup Calamata olives, pitted and cut in half

3 cloves garlic, peeled and finely chopped

1 tablespoon balsamic vinegar

2½ cups fresh ripe tomato, peeled, seeded, and cut into 1-inch cubes

¼ cup Chicken Stock (page 233) or Vegetable Stock (page 231)

2 sprigs fresh thyme

1 bay leaf

2 tablespoons finely chopped sweet basil leaves

Heat the olive oil in a large, nonstick Dutch oven or stockpot over medium heat. When hot, add the eggplant and the red and green bell peppers, and cook over medium heat for 5 minutes, stirring frequently. Add the onion and cook until it begins to turn a golden color, approximately 5 minutes. Add the zucchini, yellow squash, and olives; cook for 5 more minutes. Add the garlic and when fragrant, add the vinegar, tomato, stock, thyme, and bay leaf.

Cover and cook at very low heat for 15 more minutes. Remove the bay leaf and thyme sprigs, then stir in the basil. Cover and let rest for 5 minutes off the heat, then serve.

# Roasted Rosemary Garlic

*T*his is my mother's favorite appetizer. She eats it almost every day. She is convinced that garlic has "supernatural" qualities. It will attract love, good luck, and keep the common cold away. I especially love roasted garlic eaten with crispy French bread and butter. Buy the freshest and biggest garlic bulbs possible. Make sure that they are firm and dry, and that their paperlike skin is unbroken and tight on the bulbs. Do not rush the baking; the garlic should be tender and buttery when cooked properly.

**MAKES 4 SERVINGS**

| | |
|---|---|
| *2 large whole heads of garlic* | *4 sprigs fresh rosemary* |
| *4 tablespoons olive oil* | *Freshly ground black pepper to taste* |

Heat the oven to 375°.

Do not remove the papery outer skin from the garlic. With a very sharp knife, cut the garlic heads in half sideways. Set the garlic halves, cut side up, on a piece of aluminum foil, then drizzle each half with 1 tablespoon olive oil. Arrange the sprigs of rosemary on each half and sprinkle with pepper. Close the aluminum foil and roast for about 45 minutes, or until tender and buttery.

The garlic will be mellow and easy to spread. Serve as a side dish or as a spread for bread or rolls.

# Garlic and Onion-Roasted Potatoes

*These potatoes are excellent served with steak or any grilled or roasted meat. If you can't find tiny new potatoes, cut large potatoes into evenly sized chunks.*

**MAKES 4 SERVINGS**

1 tablespoon unsalted softened
    butter, optional
2 tablespoons olive oil
2 tablespoons balsamic vinegar
2 sprigs fresh thyme
2 sprigs fresh rosemary
½ teaspoon salt

1 teaspoon freshly ground black
    pepper
2 pounds small new red potatoes,
    1½ inches in diameter
1 whole head garlic, unpeeled, cut
    in half crosswise
1 large red onion, sliced, about
    ½ pound

Heat oven to 425°. In a baking pan, combine optional butter, oil, vinegar, herbs, salt, and pepper, and stir to mix. Add potatoes, garlic, and onion, and mix thoroughly, making sure the potatoes are coated with the mixture, and that the garlic is placed cut side down in the pan.

Cover with aluminum foil and bake in the oven for 20 minutes. Remove the foil, stir, and bake another 20 minutes, or until cooked and golden in color.

# Parisienne Potatoes

*These potatoes will surely become your favorite side dish because not only are they beautiful but also they make a delicious accompaniment to roasted meats or grilled chicken. Vary the recipe by sprinkling some finely chopped parsley and minced fresh garlic during the last 30 seconds of cooking. Or add a sprig of rosemary at the beginning of the cooking process and discard it when the potatoes are cooked. Covering the potatoes is very important; it makes them tender and moist. Don't forget to cook them very slowly and to shake the pan every 5 minutes so they will brown evenly.*

**MAKES 4 SERVINGS**

*1½ pounds large white potatoes, peeled, rinsed, and dried*
*1 tablespoon unsalted butter*

*1 tablespoon olive oil*
*Salt and freshly ground black pepper to taste*

Using a ¾-inch round (or larger) melon-ball cutter (see Note), cut the potatoes into balls. In a heavy skillet with a lid, heat the butter and olive oil. When light brown in color, add the potato balls and reduce the heat to very low. Cover and cook, shaking the pan or stirring every 5 minutes, until the potatoes are golden brown outside and tender in the center.

**NOTE:** Make the effort to use the melon-ball cutter, and resist the temptation to cut the potatoes into squares, as they will not cook as evenly and will not look as pretty. You can cut the potato balls ahead of time and hold them in cold water in the refrigerator. Save the scraps to boil and mash the next day.

# Desserts

APPLE TARTELETTE WITH WHITE-CHOCOLATE
CARAMEL SAUCE

CINNAMON ICE CREAM

SAUTÉED CINNAMON BANANAS

MAPLE AND ALMOND ZABAGLIONE WITH
MIXED BERRIES

BANANA MACADAMIA CAKE WITH MAPLE SAUCE

CHOCOLATE AND RUM TORTE

MANGO COMPOTE

WHITE CHOCOLATE CHEESECAKE

CHOCOLATE SAUCE

BLACK CHERRY CLAFOUTIS

CITRON MOUSSE

RASPBERRY COULIS

RASPBERRY CRÈME BRÛLÉE

PEAR, APPLE, AND BLACK CHERRY COBBLER

STRAWBERRY, PAPAYA, AND BANANA CRISP

BLACK CHERRY ICE CREAM

INDIVIDUAL RED BANANA CHOCOLATE CAKES

COCONUT ICE CREAM

MELTING CHOCOLATE CAKE

VANILLA–ORANGE-BLOSSOM SAUCE

KEY LIME TART

BLACK-PEPPERED STRAWBERRIES

KUMQUAT–GRAND MARNIER JAM

# Apple Tartelette

## WITH WHITE-CHOCOLATE CARAMEL SAUCE

*T*his *elegant delicious dessert can be made on the spur of the moment to serve when friends stop by informally. It should take no more than 30 minutes to prepare if you have the ice cream on hand and have already made the caramel sauce. I like these tartelettes with homemade Cinnamon Ice Cream on page 199, but you can use vanilla ice cream or frozen yogurt.*

**MAKES 4 SERVINGS**

*1 sheet frozen puff pastry, thawed*
*¼ cup sliced almonds*
*¼ cup sugar*

*4 baking apples*
*¼ cup unsalted butter, softened*

Preheat the oven to 375°. Unfold the pastry sheet, dust lightly with flour, and roll gently until ¹⁄₁₆ inch thick. Use a bowl or small dish as a pattern and cut out four 5-inch circles of puff pastry. Set the circles on a baking sheet lined with parchment paper. (Don't skip this step; it keeps the butter and sugar from sticking to the pan and burning.)

In a food processor, whirl almonds and sugar until finely ground and well mixed. Sprinkle 1 heaping teaspoon of the almond-sugar mixture onto each pastry circle.

Peel and core the apples, and cut them in half lengthwise. Lay each half on a cutting board, flat side down, and cut into thin, crosswise crescents. Brush lightly with the softened butter, then neatly arrange one sliced apple on each round of puff pastry, overlapping the slices so that they form a little mountain in the center.

Sprinkle each tartelette with the remaining almond-sugar mixture.

Bake the tartelettes in the center of the oven for about 45 to 50 minutes, until the apples are tender and golden brown.

Serve hot out of the oven, with White-Chocolate Caramel Sauce (page 198) on the bottom of the plate, and topped with a scoop of Cinnamon Ice Cream (page 199).

*(continued)*

### WHITE-CHOCOLATE CARAMEL SAUCE

*K*eeps well in the refrigerator for at least a month; to serve, scoop some into a bowl and microwave until hot. This sauce may seem tricky, but it's really not difficult to make. You just have to pay attention to it and stop the cooking process as soon as the caramel turns a dark gold.

**MAKES ABOUT 2 CUPS**

*2 cups water, divided*
*1 cup sugar*

*16 ounces white chocolate,*
*    roughly chopped*
*1 tablespoon vanilla extract*

In a heavy saucepan, bring 1 cup water and the sugar to a boil, and cook until the syrup is dark gold in color, about 8 to 9 minutes.

Remove the pan from the heat and very carefully add 1 cup cold water. The caramel may splatter, so be careful not to burn yourself.

Add the white chocolate and the vanilla, and stir over low heat until chocolate is completely melted, 2 minutes.

For a creamier, more liquid sauce, stir in ¼ to ½ cup heavy cream.

# Cinnamon Ice Cream

*F*or maximum cinnamon flavor, grate cinnamon sticks into powder (you can use a coffee grinder). There are lots of ways to make ice cream—from old-fashioned, hand-cranked freezers you fill with ice and salt to expensive electric machines. A modern, inexpensive compromise is a Donvier or other hand-turned machine that uses a liquid-filled cylinder you store in the freezer.

**MAKES 1 QUART**

| | |
|---|---|
| 2 cups heavy whipping cream | 5 egg yolks |
| 1 cup milk | ½ cup sugar |
| 1 teaspoon grated cinnamon | |

In a stainless steel saucepan, combine the cream, milk and cinnamon, and heat until scalded—tiny bubbles will form around the edge and the mixture will be steaming. Do not let it boil!

Remove from the heat, cover, and let stand 20 minutes for flavors to infuse.

Meanwhile, whisk the egg yolks and sugar in a medium bowl until thick and pale yellow in color. Return the milk mixture to the heat and bring to scalding again; be careful not to overheat. While whisking the egg mixture, slowly pour in about ½ cup of the hot milk and cream mixture and blend well.

Continue to whisk while you slowly pour in the rest of the milk and cream mixture. Pour the mixture back into the pan and cook over medium-low heat for about 10 minutes, stirring constantly with a wooden spoon, until mixture is thick enough to coat the back of a spoon. (To test, remove the spoon from the custard, turn it over, and run your finger down the back. It should leave a clear path.)

Remove from the heat and cool the mixture in an ice-water bath for 20 minutes, stirring frequently. Strain through a fine sieve, then pour into an ice cream maker and freeze according to manufacturer's directions.

The best ice cream you ever tasted!

# Sautéed Cinnamon Bananas

*Rum and banana liqueur spike a simple banana topping for ice cream.*
*Keep this recipe in mind when you have unexpected guests for dinner.*

**MAKES 4 SERVINGS**

4 ripe bananas
3 tablespoons unsalted butter,
    divided
1 teaspoon ground cinnamon
2 tablespoons brown sugar

1 tablespoon fresh lemon juice
¼ cup Crème de Banana liqueur
2 tablespoons dark rum

Cut bananas into ¼-inch diagonal slices.

In a sauté pan, heat 1 tablespoon butter and add the cinnamon, brown sugar, and lemon juice. Mix well. Add the bananas and sauté until they are soft, 2 to 3 minutes. Add the Crème de Banana and rum. When hot, add the remaining 2 tablespoons butter and serve immediately over vanilla ice cream.

# Maple and Almond Zabaglione

## WITH MIXED BERRIES

*Zabaglione is a fluffy, eggy Italian dessert sauce traditionally flavored with Marsala wine. This version is sweetened with maple syrup and flavored with almonds. It's easy to make, but don't overcook it or the mixture will collapse.*

**MAKES 4 SERVINGS**

| | |
|---|---|
| 1 pint fresh strawberries | 4 egg yolks |
| 1 pint red raspberries | ⅓ cup maple syrup |
| 1 pint black raspberries | ¼ cup Amaretto liqueur |
| | ¼ cup chopped toasted almonds |

Clean and quarter the strawberries and mix with the other berries. Divide into 4 serving dishes.

In the top of a double boiler set over, but not touching, simmering water, whisk the egg yolks, maple syrup, and Amaretto constantly until quadrupled in volume, about 5 minutes.

The mixture will become fluffy and glossy. Remove from heat, add the toasted almonds, and serve over the berries.

# Banana Macadamia Cake

## WITH MAPLE SAUCE

*T*his cake is similar to a banana bread. Cut it into very thin slices and serve them with ice cream and Maple Sauce for a delicious tropical dessert.

**MAKES 12 SERVINGS**

1 stick (4 ounces) unsalted
   butter, softened
1 cup sugar
2 eggs
1 tablespoon buttermilk
2 tablespoons coconut milk (see
   Note)
1 cup smashed bananas, about 2
   to 3 ripe bananas
¼ cup chopped macadamia nuts

¼ cup dark raisins
2 tablespoons dark rum
½ cup chopped dried banana
   chips
2 cups all-purpose flour
½ teaspoon salt
¾ teaspoon baking soda
1 teaspoon baking powder
Maple Sauce (page 203)

Heat the oven to 350°. Butter a 9 × 5 × 2½-inch loaf pan.

In a bowl, beat the butter and sugar until fluffy. Add the eggs, mix well, then add the buttermilk, coconut milk, bananas, nuts, raisins (soaked in rum for 2 minutes), the rum, and banana chips. In a separate bowl, combine the flour, salt, baking soda, and baking powder. Mix well and add to the egg and butter mixture. Blend well.

Pour into the buttered loaf pan and bake for 55 minutes. Test for doneness by inserting a small knife into the center of the loaf. If the knife blade comes out damp, bake the loaf for a few more minutes. Remove from the oven, let cool in the pan on a rack for 10 minutes, then turn out of the pan and let cool for 30 to 45 minutes.

When cool, cut the loaf into thin slices and serve with Maple Sauce and your favorite ice cream.

**NOTE:** Canned, unsweetened coconut milk is available in supermarkets. Do not buy coconut cream.

### MAPLE SAUCE

*This simple sauce uses the crème Anglaise, or basic custard technique, and should be a confidence-builder for you. Just follow the directions. You can substitute Grand Marnier or Amaretto liqueur for the bourbon.*

**MAKES 2 CUPS**

| | |
|---|---|
| *2 cups milk* | *1 teaspoon vanilla extract* |
| *4 egg yolks* | *3 tablespoons bourbon* |
| *½ cup sugar* | *2 tablespoons maple syrup* |

In a saucepan, heat the milk until it is steaming and tiny bubbles form around the edge of the pan. Do not boil the milk! In a glass bowl, whisk the egg yolks and sugar until creamy. While whisking, very slowly add the hot milk to the egg mixture.

Return the mixture to low heat on the stove and, stirring with a wooden spoon, cook until thick enough to coat the back of a spoon, 8 to 10 minutes. *Do not bring to a boil,* as the sauce will curdle. Add the vanilla, bourbon, and maple syrup, strain through a fine sieve into a bowl, and cool.

# Chocolate and Rum Torte

*To make this a layered dessert with the mango compote in the middle, half-fill a springform pan with the chocolate mixture and chill until set. Smooth on a layer of Mango Compote, then fill the rest with chocolate. Chill again. When you slice the torte, the beautiful, coral-colored mango in the middle is revealed. If you can't find bittersweet chocolate, you can substitute 7 ounces of unsweetened baking chocolate and 7 ounces of semisweet baking chocolate, but increase the sugar by ½ cup. Freeze any extra filling until firm, then scoop it out and serve with crisp sugar cookies.*

**MAKES 10 SERVINGS**

**CRUST**
¼ cup finely chopped pecans
¼ cup finely chopped almonds
½ cup chocolate wafer crumbs
4 tablespoons unsalted butter,
    melted
2 teaspoons vanilla extract

**FILLING**
10 eggs, yolks and whites
    separated

1 cup sugar
2 cups half-and-half
14 ounces bittersweet chocolate,
    chopped fine
2 envelopes unflavored gelatin
3 tablespoons dark or aged rum,
    such as Appleton
2 cups heavy whipping cream

*Make the crust:* Combine nuts, crumbs, butter, and vanilla in a bowl until well mixed. Pat into an even layer on the bottom of a buttered 9-inch springform pan. Set in refrigerator while you make the filling.

*Make the filling:* In a large, heavy-bottomed saucepan, whisk together the egg yolks and sugar until light yellow and foamy. Heat the half-and-half in another heavy-bottomed saucepan over medium heat. When hot but not boiling, stir in the chopped chocolate and stir until the chocolate is melted. Do not let the mixture boil!

While whisking, slowly pour the hot chocolate into the egg and sugar mixture. Put the saucepan on the stove over medium heat, cook and stir until hot and thickened, about 5 minutes. Stir the gelatin into the rum and add to the hot mixture. Stir well.

Put the pan in an ice bath and cool, stirring frequently. (To make an ice bath, fill a large mixing bowl about one third of the way with ice cubes and add a little water. Do not let the water slosh into the chocolate mixture.)

When the mixture has cooled and thickened, beat the egg whites until soft peaks form. In a separate bowl, whip the cream into soft peaks. Gently mix the cream into the cooled chocolate mixture, then gently fold in the egg whites. Pour the torte mixture into the springform pan and refrigerate at least 4 to 5 hours, preferably overnight.

Serve with Mango Compote.

# Mango Compote

*Cooking the mangoes for only 2 minutes preserves their delicate texture. If mangoes are not available, substitute peaches or papayas. Serve this compote with your favorite dessert, or with grilled fish or chicken.*

**MAKES ABOUT 2 CUPS**

*1 cup white Zinfandel*
*½ teaspoon ground cinnamon*

*2 cups fresh ripe mangoes, cut into ¼-inch cubes*

In a stainless steel pan, cook the wine until reduced by one half. Add the cinnamon and mangoes and cook for only 2 minutes. Let cool.

# White Chocolate Cheesecake

*This cheesecake is The Left Bank's favorite dessert. It is the lightest, creamiest, and most satisfying cheesecake you will ever make. High-quality white chocolate is often available at specialty food stores or upscale supermarkets. The Chocolate Sauce (page 208) is optional. It just gives extra pizzazz to this outstanding dessert.*

**MAKES 10 SERVINGS**

**CRUST**
1 tablespoon softened unsalted
   butter, for the pan
1 package chocolate wafers, about
   9 ounces
¼ cup almonds
1 tablespoon sugar
6 tablespoons unsalted butter,
   melted

**FILLING**
14 ounces fine-quality white
   chocolate

1 pound cream cheese, softened,
   at room temperature
4 eggs, separated
½ cup heavy whipping cream
2 tablespoons vanilla extract
1 stick (4 ounces) unsalted
   butter, softened, at room
   temperature
3 tablespoons Godiva chocolate
   liqueur
Dash salt

*Melt the chocolate:* Use a double boiler set over simmering water to melt the chocolate, stirring frequently with a wooden spoon or spatula. Remove from the heat and let cool to lukewarm.

*Make the crust:* Butter a 9-inch springform pan (see Note) with 1 tablespoon butter. Combine the chocolate wafers, almonds, and sugar in a food processor fitted with the metal blade and process until finely crushed. With the motor running, add the butter and process until well combined. Making a fist and using the back of your hand and fingers, press the mixture evenly and firmly onto the bottom and sides of the springform pan. Refrigerate the crust while you make the filling.

*Make the filling:* Preheat oven to 325°. Use an electric mixer to beat the cream cheese until smooth. On low speed, blend in the melted lukewarm chocolate and the egg yolks, 1 at a time. Scrape down the beaters, then add the cream, vanilla, butter, Godiva liqueur, and salt. Continue to beat for 2 more minutes.

In a separate bowl, use an electric mixer with clean beaters to beat the egg whites; start at low speed and increase as peaks form. When the whites are stiff but not dry, scrape them into the bowl with the filling and use a spatula to gently fold them in. Do not overmix the filling.

Pour and scrape the filling into the crust and bake approximately 1 hour, or until the cake has risen and browned slightly and just shimmers when you gently move the pan. It's a good idea to place the springform on a low, flat pan such as a pizza pan to catch dripping batter. Turn the oven off and let the cake stand in the oven for 1 more hour. Remove from the oven and cool before serving. Can be made a day ahead.

To serve, cover the bottom of a dessert plate with 2 to 3 tablespoons of optional chocolate sauce and place a cheesecake slice on top.

**NOTE:** If your springform pan has lost some of its spring, wrap the bottom and halfway up the sides with aluminum foil to prevent any dripping batter from landing on the bottom of your oven and burning.

# Chocolate Sauce

*If you use other liqueurs for the Godiva chocolate liqueur, increase the amount of chocolate. Make sure to use a quality brand of chocolate.*

**MAKES 2½ CUPS**

10 ounces semisweet dark
    chocolate
1 ½ cups heavy whipping
    cream

2 tablespoons Godiva chocolate
    liqueur
3 tablespoons sugar
3 egg yolks

In a double boiler, melt the chocolate.

In a stainless steel pan, scald the cream. Remove from the heat, add the melted chocolate and the liqueur. In a medium bowl, beat the sugar and egg yolks until pale yellow in color. Add a little of the cream and chocolate mixture and mix well. Slowly pour in the rest of the hot chocolate cream into the egg mixture.

Return the mixture to the pan and stir over medium heat for about 10 minutes. Stir constantly with a wooden spoon until mixture becomes thick enough to coat the back of a spoon. (When you run your finger across the back of the spoon, the mark of your finger should remain.) Immediately strain through a fine sieve into a bowl and whisk for a few minutes to release the heat.

# Black Cherry Clafoutis

*When I was growing up in Provence, there were two cherry trees in our backyard that gave us fruit that was big and black and so sweet. My mother used to make clafoutis—her favorite dessert—on Sunday afternoons when everyone was at home relaxing. The aroma would perfume the whole house. We could not wait for the clafoutis to cool and would eat the entire pie. This recipe is foolproof; try it and you cannot miss. You can substitute mangoes or peaches, but cherries are traditional and delicious.*

**MAKES 4 SERVINGS**

½ cup almond meal (see Note)
½ cup all-purpose flour
½ cup sugar
⅛ teaspoon salt
4 eggs
1 cup milk

1 cup heavy whipping cream
2 teaspoons vanilla extract
1 tablespoon unsalted butter
3 cups sweet black cherries, pitted
    and well drained (if canned,
    drain cherries very well)
2 tablespoons confectioners' sugar

Heat oven to 350°.

In a blender, combine the almond meal, flour, sugar, salt, eggs, milk, heavy cream, and vanilla, and blend thoroughly.

Generously butter the bottom of a 9-inch glass or ceramic baking dish. Spread the cherries evenly on the bottom of the baking dish. Pour the batter slowly over the berries. Place the dish on the center oven rack and bake for 50 minutes until puffy and golden in color. Remove from oven and dust with confectioners' sugar.

Cool before serving. Serve cold or at room temperature.

**NOTE:** To make almond meal, combine ½ cup blanched almonds and 1 tablespoon sugar in a food processor and grind until the texture is fluffy but not too fine. Do not process too long or you will have a gummy, unusable paste.

# Citron Mousse

*These mousses look like beautiful, pale yellow clouds. The Raspberry Coulis (page 211) adds sweetness and tang. A great dinner party dessert because you make it the day before serving.*

**MAKES 6 SERVINGS**

4 eggs, separated *(see* Note*)*
½ cup sugar
½ cup fresh-squeezed lemon juice
   from 2 to 3 large, juicy lemons
Zest of 1 lemon, finely grated
   *(see* Note*)*

½ cup milk
1 teaspoon vanilla extract
1 envelope unflavored gelatin
2 tablespoons water
1 teaspoon tequila
1 tablespoon lemon extract
½ cup heavy whipping cream

In a bowl, whisk together the egg yolks, sugar, lemon juice, and lemon zest until pale yellow. Set aside. Heat the milk and vanilla in a small saucepan. Do not boil. Dissolve the gelatin in water in a small bowl and stir it into the milk mixture along with the tequila.

While whisking the egg yolks, slowly pour in the hot milk mixture. Whisk in the lemon extract. Set the mixture in an ice bath (place some ice cubes in a large bowl together with a little water) to cool. Do not let the water slosh into the mousse mixture.

The mixture needs to cool until the gelatin begins to set up; it should be thick and cool before you proceed. With an electric mixer (see Note) or a balloon whisk, beat the egg whites until soft peaks form. (When you lift the beaters, the egg whites will droop, they will not be stiff.)

In a separate bowl, beat the heavy cream until soft peaks form. Stir the whipped cream slowly and gently into the chilled and thickened egg-lemon mixture. Gently fold in the egg whites.

Butter or spray with vegetable-oil cooking spray six 8-ounce soufflé or soup cups. Fill to the rim with mixture and refrigerate, preferably overnight.

To serve, run a knife around the edge of the mold, then turn onto a dessert plate. Spoon a puddle of coulis around the mousse and serve.

**NOTE:** If you have trouble separating eggs with the halves of the shells, crack an egg into your hand and let the whites drip through your fingers into a bowl. Then gently slide the yolks into another bowl. Clean hands are great, underused kitchen tools!

Grate the lemon zest before you squeeze the lemons. It's almost impossible to grate a squeezed lemon half.

Buy an extra set of beaters for your hand mixer so that you won't have to wash the beaters halfway through a recipe. Otherwise, just whip the egg whites first, then whip the cream. If you do it the other way around, the butterfat from the cream will prevent the egg whites from fluffing properly.

# Raspberry Coulis

*This is a simple fruit sauce that can be made with strawberries, blackberries, pitted cherries, or many other fruits, along with a complementary liqueur. Can be poured over ice cream or accompany the Citron Mousse (page 210), or you could just eat it plain with a spoon!*

**MAKES ABOUT 1½ CUPS**

2 cups fresh raspberries, or 1
    10-ounce package of frozen,
    thawed, and drained
    raspberries
¼ cup sugar (optional)

¼ cup orange juice
2 tablespoons lemon juice
2 tablespoons Chambord liqueur

Place berries, sugar, and orange and lemon juices in a blender, and purée until very smooth. Strain through a fine sieve into a glass bowl, pressing on the solids to extract all the juice. Stir in the Chambord, taste, and adjust the sugar to your liking.

# Raspberry Crème Brûlée

*Crème brûlée, "burnt cream," sounds exotic but all it involves is making a rich custard of egg and cream that is chilled in small dishes. The "burnt" layer is made by sprinkling the custards with sugar and then broiling or torching the sugar until it caramelizes. A small propane torch can also be used to caramelize the custard.*

**MAKES 4 SERVINGS**

6 egg yolks
½ cup, scant, sugar
2 tablespoons vanilla extract
2 cups heavy whipping cream
2 tablespoons Grand Marnier
    liqueur

1 pint fresh raspberries, or 1
    10-ounce package of frozen
    thawed, and drained
    raspberries (see Note)
4 tablespoons sugar, for topping

Combine the yolks with the sugar. Whisk until thickened and pale.

Stir the vanilla extract into the cream, and warm in a stainless steel saucepan over medium heat. Remove from the heat just before the boiling point.

Whisking all the while, slowly pour the hot cream into the egg yolks until well combined. Whisking keeps the egg yolks from scrambling. Strain the mixture through a sieve into a saucepan, return to medium-low heat and stir constantly until the mixture is thick enough to coat the back of a spoon. (To test, dip a spoon into the custard, turn it over, and run your finger down the back of the spoon. If it leaves a clear path, the custard is done.)

Stir in the Grand Marnier and remove from the heat. Place the saucepan in an ice bath (half-fill a mixing bowl or roasting pan with ice cubes and cold water) and stir frequently until the mixture cools and reaches the consistency of a very thick custard.

Sprinkle about a dozen raspberries into each of 4 small ceramic ramekins. Pour the custard over the berries and refrigerate at least 4 hours.

To serve, sprinkle about 1 tablespoon of granulated sugar over the top of each custard and place under the broiler for about 3 minutes, or until the sugar caramelizes (melts and turns light brown). Do not let the custard get too warm. If you have a propane torch, use it to caramelize the sugar on each custard. Serve immediately.

**NOTE:** You can substitute strawberries, blueberries, papayas, mangoes, peaches, or any other favorite fruit for the raspberries.

# Pear, Apple, and Black Cherry Cobbler

*For this cobbler, use pears that aren't quite ripe; the slow cooking leaves them tender and sweet. Serve it with Black Cherry Ice Cream (page 217) or best-quality commercial ice cream, like Häagen-Dazs or Ben & Jerry's. You can make your own puff pastry, but frozen puff pastry dough that is made with butter works well, too. These cobblers can be frozen before baking; just thaw in the refrigerator overnight, then bake for about 30 minutes. You'll need 6 individual ceramic ramekins or other ovenproof bowls, 4 to 5 inches in diameter and 1½ inches deep.*

**MAKES 6 SERVINGS**

*1 bottle white Zinfandel wine*
*2 Bartlett or Bosc pears, peeled, halved, cored, and cut into ½-inch cubes*
*2 Granny Smith apples, peeled, halved, cored, and cut into ½-inch cubes*
*¼ cup fresh lemon juice*
*¼ cup sugar*

*¼ teaspoon ground cinnamon*
*1 can (about 1 pound) pitted black cherries in heavy syrup*
*1 sheet (about ¾ pound), frozen thawed puff pastry*
*1 tablespoon sugar*
*2 tablespoons chopped, blanched almonds*

In a stainless steel saucepan, bring the wine to a boil and cook until volume is reduced by two thirds. Add pears, apples, and juice from canned cherries, and cook at medium to low heat for 15 to 20 minutes until fruit is tender. Add the lemon juice, sugar, cinnamon, and cherries, and cook for 2 to 3 more minutes. Drain the fruit through a colander and reserve the cooking liquid. Return the liquid to the saucepan and cook until it becomes syrupy and only about ¾ cup remains.

Heat the oven to 400°.

Working on a lightly floured surface, roll out the pastry into pieces about ¹⁄₁₆-inch thick and large enough to cover the baking dishes. Portion the fruit among the dishes and then divide the syrup equally among them. Cover each dish with the dough, press firmly around the edge of the dish, and trim neatly with a sharp knife. With a small, sharp knife, cut slits in the pastry in a decorative pattern.

Combine sugar and almonds in a mini-food processor and pulse to blend. Sprinkle each dish with the sugar-almond mixture. Bake for 15 to 20 minutes, or until golden brown. Serve with vanilla ice cream.

# Strawberry, Papaya, and Banana Crisp

*This tropical fruit cobbler is a 90s-style dessert that's easy to make and absolutely delicious. Use other combinations of fruit if you like, and for family dining, make it in a 9- by 13-inch glass baking dish. Serve it with the Coconut Ice Cream (page 219) in this book or with purchased vanilla ice cream or frozen yogurt.*

**MAKES 6 SERVINGS**

### TOPPING
¾ cup all-purpose flour
⅓ cup granulated sugar
⅓ cup light brown sugar
½ teaspoon ground cinnamon
Pinch salt
4 tablespoons unsalted butter, cut
   into small cubes
1 tablespoon vanilla extract

### FRUIT MIXTURE
2 cups chopped strawberries
2 cups chopped papaya
2 cups chopped bananas
2 tablespoons unsalted butter,
   softened but not melted
½ cup sugar
1 tablespoon vanilla extract
3 tablespoons cornstarch dissolved
   in 3 tablespoons rum

Heat oven to 375°.

*Make the topping:* In a glass bowl, mix the flour, sugars, cinnamon, and salt. When mixed, incorporate the butter and vanilla. The mixture should look coarse and small beads of butter should remain. You can also do this in a food processor.

*Make the fruit mixture:* In a glass bowl, mix all ingredients gently. Divide the fruit mixture into individual 6-ounce ovenproof soup cups. Spread the topping evenly over the fruit. Bake on the center rack of the oven for 25 minutes, or until the tops are golden and crisp.

Let rest for 15 minutes and serve with Coconut Ice Cream.

# Black Cherry Ice Cream

*Try using a vanilla bean instead of vanilla extract in this delicious dessert. Vanilla beans are long and thin, sold in jars, and are found in supermarkets or in specialty food stores. After use, rinse and dry the vanilla bean and bury it in a small container of sugar to infuse it with wonderful aroma and flavor. Use the vanilla sugar in baking.*

**MAKES 1 QUART**

2 cups heavy whipping cream
¾ cup milk
1 vanilla bean, split lengthwise
5 egg yolks
½ cup sugar

2 tablespoons Kirsch liqueur
½ cup black cherries, pitted and drained (use canned cherries if fresh cherries aren't in season)

Combine the cream, milk, and vanilla bean in a stainless steel saucepan, and heat to scalding. Little bubbles will appear around the edges of the pan. Do not boil! Remove the pan from the heat, cover, and let it stand for 20 minutes so that the flavors can infuse.

In a medium bowl, whisk the egg yolks and sugar until thick and pale yellow in color. Return the milk mixture to the stove and heat again to scalding. Add the Kirsch and do not let the mixture boil.

While whisking the egg mixture, slowly pour in about ½ cup of the hot milk. Then, stirring constantly, slowly pour the rest of the hot milk into the egg mixture.

Pour the custard back into the saucepan and cook over medium-low heat for about 10 minutes, stirring constantly with a wooden spoon, until the mixture thickens enough to coat the back of the spoon. (To test, remove the spoon from the custard, turn it over and run your finger down the back. It should leave a clear path.)

Remove the thickened custard from the stove and cool in an ice bath for 20 minutes. Strain through a fine sieve and then pour into an ice cream maker and churn according to manufacturer's directions.

When the ice cream is almost as thick as you want it, add the drained and pitted black cherries and finish freezing.

# Individual Red Banana Chocolate Cakes

*T*he technique of this recipe is unusual but simple. The results are exotic and delicious . . . individual hot, creamy chocolate cakes with a middle layer of melting bananas. As a bonus, the molds can be made ahead and refrigerated. Then at serving time, microwave them for 45 seconds on medium heat to soften the butter and chocolate on the inside. Serve with Coconut Ice Cream (page 219). Perfect for a dinner party.

**MAKES 6 SERVINGS**

1 cup whole blanched almonds
1 cup sugar
8 egg whites
½ cup all-purpose flour
7 ounces (1 stick plus 6 tablespoons) unsalted butter, melted

¼ cup cocoa powder
2 tablespoons vanilla extract
1 tablespoon Godiva chocolate liqueur, optional
2 medium-ripe red bananas (or yellow bananas)

In a food processor fitted with the metal blade, grind together the almonds and sugar until they are of uniform texture. (Almonds ground alone turn to nut butter.) In a stainless steel saucepan, combine the almond-sugar mixture and egg whites. Stir and cook over medium heat for just a few minutes until the mixture begins to foam. Remove from the heat, then stir in the flour, melted butter, and cocoa. Stir in the vanilla and liqueur, if using. Let the batter cool for at least 30 minutes.

Lavishly butter six 4-ounce ceramic ramekins or metal baking molds. Fill them halfway with the batter, then let them rest for about 15 minutes.

Meanwhile, heat oven to 350°. Slice the bananas ¼ inch thick and lay 4 or 5 slices in each mold. Fill the molds to the top with the remaining batter, place in a baking pan, and bake for 20 minutes. Remove from the oven and let cool for 5 minutes. Unmold. If you wish, serve immediately with the Coconut Ice Cream or rum crème Anglaise. Or let molds cool, cover, and refrigerate until serving time. To prepare for serving, place 1 molded dessert on a plate and microwave on high for 45 seconds.

# Coconut Ice Cream

*Once you have tried this recipe, you will never again buy ice cream from the store. It's an excellent accompaniment to many of the desserts in this book and makes a great milk shake.*

**MAKES 1 QUART**

2 cups heavy whipping cream
¾ cup milk
½ cup unsweetened coconut milk

1 teaspoon vanilla extract
5 egg yolks
½ cup sugar

In a stainless steel saucepan, combine the cream, milk, and coconut milk, and heat until scalded—tiny bubbles will form around the edge and the mixture will be steaming. Do not allow it to boil!

Remove from the heat and add the vanilla.

Meanwhile, whisk the egg yolks and sugar in a medium bowl until thick and pale yellow in color. While whisking the egg mixture, slowly pour in about ½ cup of the hot milk and mix well.

Continue to whisk while you slowly pour in the rest of the milk and cream mixture. Pour the mixture back into the pan and cook over medium-low heat for about 10 minutes, stirring constantly with a wooden spoon, until mixture is thick enough to coat the back of a spoon.

To test, remove the spoon from the custard, turn it over, and run your finger down the back. It should leave a clear path.

Remove from the heat and cool mixture in an ice bath for 20 minutes. Strain through a fine sieve, then pour into an ice cream maker, and freeze according to manufacturer's directions.

# Melting Chocolate Cake

*I can hear you saying, "This has got to be the best chocolate dessert I have ever tasted in my life!" Just be sure to buy the best-quality semisweet chocolate you can find. And bake the molds only about 10 minutes, as the center should be very runny. Pour the vanilla-orange sauce over the chocolate custard for a sensational taste treat.*

**MAKES 6 SERVINGS**

8 ounces (2 sticks) unsalted butter
8 ounces semisweet chocolate
4 egg yolks

5 whole eggs
1 cup sugar
1 cup (slightly heaping) all-purpose flour

Heat the oven to 450°.

In the top of a double boiler set over but not in simmering water, melt the butter and chocolate. Using a wooden spoon, stir continuously to help the process along.

In a glass bowl, whip the egg yolks, the whole eggs, and the sugar until tripled in volume. When the chocolate mixture is fully melted, whisk it into the egg mixture.

When all the ingredients are well incorporated, whisk in the flour, making sure there are no lumps.

Generously butter six 6-ounce metal molds. Pour the batter into the molds, up to ¼ inch from top. Bake in the oven for about 10 minutes. Unmold and serve immediately.

# Vanilla–Orange-Blossom Sauce

*This is a vanilla custard sauce flavored with orange. If you have difficulty finding orange flower water, just prepare the sauce without it. It will still be an excellent dessert sauce, with a hint of orange from the zest.*

**MAKES ABOUT 2 CUPS**

*1½ cup heavy whipping cream*
*Grated zest from 1 orange*
*2 tablespoons orange blossom/ orange flower water*

*1 vanilla bean, split lengthwise*
*3 tablespoons sugar*
*3 egg yolks*

In a stainless steel pan, heat the cream, orange zest, orange blossom water, and vanilla bean until hot and steaming; do not boil.

Remove from the heat, cover, and let the flavors infuse for 20 minutes. In a medium bowl, beat the sugar and egg yolks until pale yellow in color. Add a little of the hot mixture to the egg mixture and mix well.

Slowly whisk the rest of the cream mixture into the egg mixture. Pour into the stainless steel pan and return to medium heat for about 10 minutes. Stir constantly with a wooden spoon until mixture becomes thick enough to coat the back of a spoon. (When you run your finger across the back of a spoon, the mark of your finger should remain.)

Immediately strain through a fine strainer into a bowl and whisk it for a few minutes to release the heat.

# Key Lime Tart

*Florida's Key lime pie is famous. This is as close as you can get to the real McCoy without preparing your own pastry crust. The pie contains no gelatin; the egg yolks and lime juice create a beautifully balanced, sweet yet tart dessert. The pie is very simple to prepare; just follow all the directions carefully. And please do not use bottled Key lime juice. If you cannot find true Key limes (named for Florida's Keys), Tahitian or Haitian limes are just fine.*

**MAKES 1 9-INCH TART TO SERVE 8**

**CRUST**
1 cup graham cracker crumbs
½ cup grated coconut
¼ cup unsalted butter, melted
¼ cup finely chopped almonds

**FILLING**
4 egg yolks
14 ounces sweetened condensed
   milk

½ cup freshly squeezed lime juice
1 teaspoon grated orange zest

**MERINGUE TOPPING**
4 egg whites
¼ teaspoon cream of tartar
½ cup superfine sugar (see Note)

*Make the crust:* In a bowl, mix all ingredients until well blended. Press mixture onto bottom and sides of a 9- or 10-inch tart pan with a removable bottom. Set tart shell in refrigerator.

*Make the filling:* Separate the egg yolks and whites and set the whites aside in a clean, small mixing bowl. When you're ready to make the meringue, they'll be at room temperature and ready to beat.

Whisk or stir the egg yolks and condensed milk together until creamy. Gradually drizzle in the lime juice and orange zest, stirring gently to combine. The mixture will take on a milky-opaque look. Pour and scrape the filling into the tart shell and return to the refrigerator for at least 1 hour.

*Make the meringue:* Heat oven to 375°. Beat the egg whites to soft peaks. Add the cream of tartar. Continue to beat while slowly adding the sugar; beat until mixture is stiff. Spread the meringue over the pie, being sure it covers all of the filling, and bake until golden brown on top, about 10 minutes. Remove the pan from the oven and set on a rack to cool. When the tart is cool to the touch, remove the sides from the tart pan and set it on a serving platter.

**NOTE:** You can find superfine sugar in liquor stores and some supermarkets. You can also whirl regular sugar in a food processor or blender. Do not use powdered sugar.

# Black-Peppered Strawberries

*You might think that black pepper and strawberries are an odd couple. Would I steer you wrong? To make this dessert even more special, sprinkle ¼ teaspoon of superior-quality balsamic vinegar on top.*

**MAKES 4 SERVINGS**

2 tablespoons unsalted butter
3 cups chopped ripe strawberries
Zest from 1 orange, sliced in very
    fine strips
¼ cup fresh orange juice

2 tablespoons Grand Marnier or
    orange liqueur, optional
2 teaspoons finely cracked black
    peppercorns
¼ teaspoon ground cinnamon

In a sauté pan, heat the butter and when foamy, add the strawberries. Sauté for 1 minute. Add the orange zest, orange juice and Grand Marnier, if using. Reduce the heat, add the peppercorns and cinnamon, and cook for 5 more minutes.

Serve hot on top of vanilla ice cream in a large dessert glass.

# Kumquat Grand Marnier Jam

*The day I bought my house in Fort Lauderdale, I saw a huge kumquat tree in the middle of my backyard and thought that it was an orange tree filled with baby oranges. This pygmy of the citrus family looks like a tiny oval or round orange. You can find fresh kumquats only once a year, around Christmas. If they are not available, use tangerines and reduce the sugar.*

**MAKES 3 CUPS**

1 pound kumquats, peeled and
    seeded
1 tablespoon unsalted butter
1 tablespoon minced shallots
1 tablespoon minced onion
1 cup orange segments, chopped
    and seeded, white skin
    removed
1 cup tangerine segments,
    chopped and seeded, white
    skin removed

½ cup orange juice
½ cup sugar
¼ cup Grand Marnier or other
    orange liqueur
¼ teaspoon ground cinnamon
¼ teaspoon ground cloves
¼ teaspoon ground ginger
Salt and freshly ground black
    pepper

Quarter the kumquats. In a saucepan, heat the butter, add the shallots and onions, and cook until translucent, not brown. Add the kumquats, orange and tangerine segments, orange juice, sugar, Grand Marnier, cinnamon, cloves, and ginger. Bring to a boil, reduce heat to low, cover, and cook for 10 minutes. Adjust the salt and pepper to taste.

Serve hot with pork tenderloin or grilled chicken. The jam keeps refrigerated for up to 3 weeks.

# Stocks and Other Basics

VEGETABLE STOCK

SHELLFISH STOCK

CHICKEN STOCK

DUCK STOCK

BROWN BEEF STOCK


BASIC MAYONNAISE

AIOLI

CHILI MAYONNAISE

CHIVE CRÈME FRAÎCHE

ALMOND PESTO


FRESH HERB OILS

CHIVE OIL

ARUGULA OIL

BLACK OLIVE OIL

DRIED CHILI OIL

DRIED SPICE OIL

ROASTED GARLIC OIL

# STOCKS

Making your own chicken stock, vegetable broth, or beef stock is easy. And the taste is so delicious.

You don't have to make stocks every week to master Sunshine Cuisine, but if you devote a little effort just two or three days a year, then you'll have the makings of wonderful sauces. Just freeze them in ice cube trays. That way, when you need ¼ cup of beef stock to finish a sauce, just pop a couple of cubes into the microwave to melt, and you're cooking.

Making stocks sounds mysterious and difficult, but don't be afraid. All it involves is a few pounds of bones, veal or chicken, usually, cooked in water over low heat with vegetables, herbs, and seasonings for a long time until everything gives up its delicious flavors to the liquid.

You can start a beef stock in the late afternoon on a Saturday, then let it simmer overnight. In the morning, turn the heat off, let the stock cool, then strain the stock and pack it away in the freezer. For just a little effort, you get a huge payback in flavor.

Once you've made your own stocks, compare their big taste to what you can get in a can and, I promise, you'll be a believer.

Here are a few tricks of the trade to make your stocks a breeze:

- Always start with cold water and bring stocks to a boil very gradually. This prevents clouding and the low heat helps extract the maximum amount of flavor from the ingredients.

- Don't be tempted to cook stocks at a brisk boil for a shorter time. They should simmer gently—bubble very slowly—for best results.

- Don't tie up herbs and seasonings in cheesecloth before adding them to a stock. They'll be strained out later.

- For beef stock, leave the onion peels on for a deeper color. For chicken or vegetable stock, peel the onions.

- Remove the leaves from celery stalks; they turn bitter during long cooking.

- Tomatoes add a subtle but delicious flavor to stocks, so don't leave them out.

- Rinse leeks well to remove the grit between the layers. Use both the tender white bottoms and the tougher green tops.

- Use whole peppercorns instead of ground pepper so your stocks won't be speckled. Do not salt stocks. It's better to add salt to individual dishes than to risk making a stock too salty after being reduced (cooked down).

- The longer a stock has to cook, the larger the pieces of vegetables should be. For a quick-cooking vegetable stock, cut the vegetables into small pieces. For a long-cooking beef stock, leave the vegetables in large chunks.

# Vegetable Stock

*This is a light, flavorful vegetable broth for use in soup and sauce making. It can be made, start to finish, in 1 hour.*

**MAKES 2 QUARTS**

2 tablespoons olive oil
1 large onion, peeled and sliced
2 large shallots, peeled and
    chopped
2 large carrots, scrubbed and cut
    into ½-inch chunks
2 celery stalks, cut into ½-inch
    chunks (remove leaves)
1 turnip, chopped, optional
1 large tomato, cut into large
    chunks
2 garlic cloves, peeled and
    crushed

1 leek, washed of any grit, cut
    into ½-inch pieces (use both
    green and white parts)
3 quarts (12 cups) cold water
3 sprigs fresh parsley, including
    stems
2 sprigs fresh thyme
1 large bay leaf
6 whole peppercorns
1 teaspoon fennel seeds, optional
3 whole cloves, optional

Put olive oil into a large stockpot over medium heat, then add onion and shallots, and cook until translucent and wilted, about 5 minutes. Do not let onion brown. Add the remaining vegetables and cook until the vegetables begin to "sweat," or release their juices, 5 to 10 minutes. Stir, using a wooden spoon. Add the water and seasonings, bring to a boil, then reduce heat so that broth just simmers—bubbles gently—and cook it for 40 minutes. Strain the vegetable stock through a fine sieve, then strain again, this time through a sieve or colander lined with a double layer of cheesecloth. Let cool, then transfer into 1- and 2-cup containers for freezing. Label and date containers.

The broth will keep for 2 to 3 days in the refrigerator, for about 3 months in the freezer.

# Shellfish Stock

*This stock is so sweet and flavorful that you will want to use it all the time. The lobster and shrimp shells may be hard to find. Ask your fish supplier or favorite restaurant; they may have some to share with you.*

**MAKES 1 QUART**

2 tablespoons olive oil
3 pounds lobster and shrimp
   shells
2 medium onions, peeled and
   finely chopped
1 leek, cleaned and finely chopped
2 carrots, peeled and finely
   chopped
2 celery stalks, finely chopped
2 tomatoes, cut into small sections

3 sprigs fresh parsley, including
   stems
3 sprigs fresh thyme
2 sprigs fresh tarragon
1 large bay leaf
6 white peppercorns
1 teaspoon fennel seeds
1½ quarts water
1 cup dry white wine
¼ cup tomato paste

In a large stockpot, heat the olive oil and sauté the shells for 2 minutes. Add all the vegetables and cook until they "sweat," for 2 minutes. Add the herbs and seasonings, and the water, wine, and tomato paste. Stir, and cook for 20 minutes on low heat. Strain and use immediately or freeze. The stock will keep a day in the refrigerator or a month in the freezer.

# Chicken Stock

*Tomatoes, leeks, and fresh herbs add a depth of flavor to this delicious, rich chicken stock. This is one of* Sunshine Cuisine's *most-used basic stocks.*

**MAKES 2 QUARTS**

4 pounds chicken bones and parts (back, neck, carcasses, thighs)
3 quarts cold water
2 medium onions, peeled and chopped coarsely
1 leek, rinsed well to remove sand, cut into ½-inch pieces (use both green and white parts)

2 carrots, scrubbed and cut into ½-inch chunks
2 celery stalks, cut into ½-inch chunks (remove leaves)
2 tomatoes, cut into chunks
3 sprigs fresh parsley, including stems
3 sprigs fresh thyme
1 large bay leaf
6 whole peppercorns

Rinse the chicken parts in cold water, then put them in a large stockpot (see Note). Add the water, then place the pot over medium-low heat and slowly bring to a boil. This will help prevent the stock from clouding. Do not cover the pot. When the stock is boiling, reduce the heat so that it simmers—bubbles gently—and skim the froth and foam from the surface, using a slotted spoon.

Let simmer for about 4 hours, skimming as needed. After 4 hours, add the vegetables, herbs, and spices, and cook 1 more hour. Turn off the heat and let the stock cool for 30 minutes to 1 hour. Use a slotted spoon to remove the chicken bones—the meat will have fallen off the bone by now—and discard them. Then, strain the stock through a fine sieve and discard the vegetables left behind. Strain again, this time through a sieve or colander lined with a double layer of cheesecloth. Divide the stock into various-size freezer containers, let cool a while longer, then freeze.

It's a good idea to freeze some of the stock in ice cube trays. Then, store the frozen cubes in a plastic bag or freezer container. Each cube is about 2 tablespoons, very useful when you need only a little stock to make a pan sauce.

*(continued)*

The stock will keep for 2 to 3 days in the refrigerator, 3 to 6 months in the freezer.

**NOTE:** Don't remove the fat and skin from the chicken before cooking. That's where much of the flavor lies, and fat helps form a seal to keep stock fresh in the refrigerator or freezer. Later, it's easy to lift off the layer of fat from the chilled stock before adding the stock to a recipe.

Save chicken parts in the freezer until you have enough to make stock, but blanch them first to remove any flavors the bones may have picked up in the freezer. Put the parts in a stockpot, cover with water, and bring to a boil. Then, drain the water and rinse the chicken parts to remove any debris. Then start the recipe, again using cold water.

# Duck Stock

1 roasted carcass plus uncooked
  neck, wing tips, and giblets
  from a 4½- to
  5-pound duck
2 medium onions, peeled and
  quartered
2 medium carrots, peeled and cut
  into 1-inch pieces

2 sprigs fresh thyme
2 sprigs fresh rosemary
2 bay leaves
1 leek, washed and cut into
  1-inch pieces
12 whole black peppercorns
3 celery stalks, cut into 1-inch
  pieces

Remove the rack from the roasting pan and discard all excess fat. Chop the roasted duck carcass into 4 to 5 pieces (remove and discard the orange, apple, and onion in the cavity) and place in roasting pan with the reserved neck, wing tips, and giblets. Add the onions and carrots. Roast at 400° for 30 to 45 minutes until lightly browned. Pour off excess fat and transfer all ingredients to a stockpot.

Add enough water to cover, about 10 cups. Add 1 cup of water to the roasting pan and set over medium-high heat on the stovetop. Bring to a boil, scraping the pan bottom of any browned bits, and add these juices and bits to the stockpot. Add the thyme, rosemary, bay leaves, leek, black peppercorns, and celery. Bring to a boil.

Skim any scum from the surface, reduce the heat to low and let simmer, uncovered, for about 2 hours. Be sure to skim the surface every 30 minutes. Strain the stock through a very fine sieve and return to a clean saucepan and cook until only 3 cups are left. The stock can be covered and refrigerated for up to 1 week and frozen up to 6 months.

# Brown Beef Stock

*This stock takes a long time, from start to finish, but most of the cooking is unsupervised. Make it on a day when you have a lot to do in your house, or time the cooking so the stock simmers overnight.*

**MAKES 2 QUARTS**

2 tablespoons vegetable oil
4 pounds beef bones
1 pound veal trimmings
    (optional; not needed if bones
    are very meaty)
2 medium onions, unpeeled, cut
    into chunks
1 leek, rinsed well to remove grit,
    cut into 1-inch pieces (use
    both white and green parts)

2 carrots, scrubbed and cut into
    1-inch pieces
2 celery stalks, cut into 1-inch
    pieces (remove leaves)
2 tomatoes, cut into 8 wedges
3 sprigs fresh parsley, including
    stems
3 sprigs fresh thyme
1 large bay leaf
6 whole black peppercorns

Heat oven to 400°.

Place a large roasting pan on the stove, over 2 burners if pan is very large, add oil, and heat over medium flame. Place the bones in the pan in a single layer and cook, turning with tongs, until golden brown on all sides. This will take 5 to 10 minutes. Add veal trimmings, if using, scattering them through the pan, and place the roasting pan in the oven. Let the bones cook for 1½ hours. Remove the roasting pan from the oven and place browned bones in a large stockpot. Add 2 quarts of cold water.

Place the roasting pan on the stove, add the vegetables to the brown bits and fat, and cook over medium heat for 10 to 15 minutes until vegetables have browned and caramelized. Stir often to prevent burning, scraping the pan with a wooden spoon to loosen the tasty brown bits.

Pour and scrape everything into the stockpot with the browned bones. Add enough water to cover all ingredients by 2 inches. Add herbs and seasonings. Bring to a boil, then reduce the heat so that the mixture just bubbles at a gentle simmer, and let cook for 8 to 12 hours, or overnight. Turn off the heat and let the stock cool for 2 hours, stirring occasionally to release the heat.

Don't worry about removing the fat floating on top of the stock. It helps keep the stock fresh by forming a seal in the refrigerator or freezer; you can remove it later before you reheat the stock.

When the stock has cooled a bit, use a slotted spoon or tongs to remove the bones and discard. Strain the stock through a fine sieve, then strain again through a sieve or colander lined with a double thickness of cheesecloth to remove any small particles (see Note).

Portion the stock into ice cube trays or into pint or quart containers and let cool. Label and date containers, then freeze.

**NOTE:** Once you've made a nice brown beef stock, you can easily turn it into a demiglaze. Simply cook the strained stock in a large saucepan until its volume has reduced by half and it forms a syrupy liquid. This takes up less room in the refrigerator or freezer, and it's easy to scoop out a tablespoon or two as you need it.

If you'd like to produce a true glace de viande, or meat glaze, transfer the demiglaze into a smaller saucepan and again cook gently until the volume has reduced by half. When cooled, this will form a gelatinous mixture that has an extremely concentrated flavor. I recommend that you just use the demiglaze.

# About Mayonnaise

*H*omemade mayonnaise is so easy to prepare, and its taste is superior to the store-bought kind. It takes only 10 minutes, a few utensils, a few ingredients, and a little patience to make a homemade mayonnaise—the most mellow and mouth-watering imaginable.

Here are the secrets to making good mayonnaise:

1. Temperature of the ingredients—everything must be at room temperature. After all, mayonnaise originated in the south of France, where the weather is hot, so the sauce is sensitive to cold. If you use cold or hot ingredients or utensils, the mayonnaise could "break," or curdle.

2. Proportion of oil to egg yolks—1 large egg yolk will absorb about ¾ cup oil. If you use more oil than that, the yolk becomes so saturated, it loses its binding properties and the mayonnaise could thin or separate.

3. How the oil is added to the egg yolks and seasonings—this is the only tricky part. The oil must literally be added drop by drop until the mayonnaise is thick and glossy and holding together in an emulsion. You can't take any short-cuts. If you try to speed up the process, the mayonnaise will refuse to thicken. All the while you're adding the oil, you must keep briskly whisking the mixture. As the mayonnaise thickens and turns glossy, add the oil a bit faster—in a steady trickle—while whisking.

*Fixing a "broken" mayonnaise:* Suppose your mayonnaise does separate. Don't panic. And don't throw it out. Just beat a fresh yolk in another bowl and gradually whisk in the "broken" mayonnaise as you would the oil. Nothing but a little time is lost.

Of course, there is a way to make mayonnaise even more quickly—by using a blender or food processor. But then you need to use the white of the egg (for proper consistency) and that diminishes the richness of the mayonnaise.

Follow these simple instructions and you'll have foolproof mayonnaise.

# Basic Mayonnaise

**MAKES 2 CUPS**

*2 egg yolks*
*1 tablespoon Dijon mustard*
*¼ teaspoon salt*
*¼ teaspoon white pepper*

*1½ cups sunflower oil*
*1 tablespoon lemon juice*
*2 tablespoons white wine vinegur*

Place the egg yolks in a glass bowl or 4-cup glass measure. Add mustard, salt, and pepper, and whisk together briefly. Begin adding 1 cup of the oil, almost drop by drop, while whisking continuously. When the mixture begins to thicken, whisk in the oil in a thin stream. Then whisk in the lemon juice and vinegar. This will dilute the mixture slightly. Continue to add the remaining oil, beginning in a thin stream, then increase the flow as the sauce thickens.

# Aioli

4 garlic cloves, peeled
5 dashes Tabasco sauce
1 capful white wine

Worcestershire sauce
1 cup mayonnaise

Put the garlic cloves through a garlic press, then whisk into the mayonnaise along with the Tabasco and Worcestershire sauce. (Use white Worcestershire sauce so the mayonnaise keeps its pale color.) Adjust the seasoning, if desired. Cover with wet wax paper or plastic wrap and refrigerate. Refrigerated, the mayonnaise will keep for 2 to 3 days.

# Chili Mayonnaise

*If you cannot find cayenne and serrano peppers, fingerhot peppers and jalapeños will work as well.*

MAKES 1 CUP

1 sliced fresh cayenne pepper,
  seeds and ribs removed
1 sliced fresh serrano pepper,
  seeds and ribs removed

2 cloves garlic, peeled
2 tablespoons fresh lemon juice
1 cup mayonnaise

Combine peppers, garlic, and lemon juice in a food processor or blender, and purée until very smooth.

In a glass bowl, mix the pepper mixture with the mayonnaise.

# Chive Crème Fraîche

*Crème fraîche has a slightly tangy, slightly nutty flavor that's wonderful. It's easy to make at home and will keep for a couple of weeks in the refrigerator. Crème fraîche is used in cooking, too, because it doesn't separate when heated as sour cream does.*

**MAKES 1 CUP**

1 cup heavy whipping cream (not ultrapasteurized)
1 tablespoon buttermilk
¼ teaspoon salt

1 tablespoon freshly chopped chives
¼ teaspoon ground white pepper

In a large glass bowl, mix together the cream, buttermilk, and salt. Cover the bowl with plastic wrap and let stand at room temperature for 24 to 36 hours. The cream will thicken, become very creamy, and develop a smooth nutlike flavor.

Refrigerate for 24 more hours for more texture and flavor. Add the chives and white pepper, and mix well.

# Almond Pesto

*I love to make pesto with almonds instead of the traditional pine nuts. Almonds are more flavorful, and they do not have a starchy taste. A blend of fresh basil and cilantro gives the pesto a very definite character. You can use this pesto in soups, for pastas, grilled chicken, or fish.*

**MAKES 2 CUPS**

4 garlic cloves, peeled and
    chopped
½ cup blanched almonds
1 tablespoon balsamic vinegar
1 cup tightly packed fresh sweet
    basil leaves
1 cup tightly packed fresh cilantro
    leaves

½ cup freshly grated Parmigiano-
    Reggiano cheese
½ cup freshly grated Romano
    cheese
¼ teaspoon freshly ground black
    pepper
1 cup extra-virgin olive oil

Chop the garlic and almonds together in a food processor, then add the vinegar, basil, and cilantro. Pulse to chop the herbs and combine the ingredients. Now, add the cheeses and pepper, and pulse to blend. Then, with the motor running, slowly pour in enough oil to make a paste. You might not use the entire cup of oil.

# Fresh Herb Oils

*These are my favorite oils for salads, grilled fish and seafood, and pork and lamb chops. You can buy flavored oils in specialty food stores, but they're easy to make at home and cost much less. When the herbed oils are gently warmed, their flavors intensify.*

| FOR THIS HERB: | USE THIS OIL: |
|---|---|
| Basil | Extra-virgin olive oil |
| Cilantro | Extra-virgin olive oil |
| Chervil | Sunflower oil |
| Mint | Grape-seed oil |

In 4 cups of boiling water, combine 1 tablespoon baking soda, 1 tablespoon white wine vinegar, and 1 cup tightly packed herb of your choice. Leave the herb in water only for 15 seconds to preserve the color. Rinse the herb under cold running water and squeeze out excess water.

Put the herb into a blender with 1 cup of the appropriate oil. Blend well. Pour into a bottle and add 1 additional cup of oil. Blend well, shaking vigorously, and leave on the kitchen counter (*not in the sunlight*) for 2 hours, then refrigerate. These oils do not stay green for a long time, so use them within a few days.

# Chive Oil

Follow the instructions on page 243 for Fresh Herb Oils, using the same method with 24 to 30 chives with grape-seed oil. Refrigerate and use within a few days.

# Arugula Oil

Follow the instructions on page 243 for Fresh Herb Oils, using the same method with 2 cups of arugula with grape-seed oil. Refrigerate and use within a few days.

# Black Olive Oil

*1 packed cup Calamata olives,*
*pitted*
*¼ cup water*

*2 cups extra-virgin olive oil*

In a saucepan over medium heat, reduce (cook down) the olives and water until all water has evaporated. In a blender, add the olives and olive oil and blend well. Pour into a bottle and refrigerate. Let the oil "age" for a couple of days before using. This very fruity oil will last in the refrigerator for 2 to 3 months.

# Dried Chili Oil

*¼ cup dried chili flakes*
*¼ cup water*

*2 cups extra-virgin olive oil*

In a saucepan over medium heat, combine the chili flakes and water. Bring to a boil and cook until all liquid evaporates. Add the oil, pour into a bottle, and let sit on kitchen counter for 2 days. Shake the bottle from time to time. Do not strain the oil, but leave the chili flakes in the bottom of the bottle. This oil will stay good for 6 months.

# Dried Spice Oil

*The beautiful colors of homemade spice and herb oils deserve beautiful containers. So save oil, vinegar, wine and liquor bottles with pleasing shapes or look for interesting bottles at garage sales and antiques shops. You can also buy reproduction pressed-glass bottles in cookware shops.*

| FOR THIS SPICE: | USE THIS OIL: |
|---|---|
| Ginger | Extra-virgin olive oil |
| Curry | Peanut oil |
| Paprika | Grape-seed oil |
| Coriander | Grape-seed oil |
| Cayenne | Extra-virgin olive oil |
| Nutmeg | Peanut oil |
| Mustard | Grape-seed oil |
| Saffron | Grape-seed oil |

Mix 2 tablespoons of any one of the spices with ½ cup of water in a small saucepan. Bring to a boil over medium heat and cook until ¼ cup remains. Add the appropriate oil, mix well, pour into a bottle, and leave on the kitchen counter for 2 days, shaking the bottle often to intensify the flavor of the spice.

Strain the oil through a coffee filter or a very fine cheesecloth. Do not pour the remaining solids at the bottom of the bottle through the filter. The oil can be kept at room temperature for up to 3 months without any loss of flavor.

# Roasted Garlic Oil

*Be sure to refrigerate these wonderful oils so they don't grow any dangerous bacteria. The oil may congeal in the refrigerator, but if you take it out for a while before you need it, the olive oil will "melt" again.*

*4 large whole heads of garlic with
  tight, papery skins*

*4 cups extra-virgin olive oil plus
  4 tablespoons*

Heat oven to 375°.

With a very sharp knife, cut the unpeeled garlic head in half crosswise. Set the halves side by side on a piece of aluminum foil, then drizzle with the 4 tablespoons of olive oil.

Close the aluminum foil very tightly and roast in the oven for about 20 minutes.

Remove from the oven and let stand until cool enough to handle. Squeeze the garlic cloves from their skins and place in a jar or bottle. Add the remaining olive oil. Shake well and refrigerate. The oil is ready in a few days and will keep for up to 3 weeks.

**GARLIC OIL**

*½ cup peeled garlic cloves*

*4 cups extra-virgin olive oil,
  divided*

In a blender, purée the garlic cloves with 1 cup of the oil to make a paste. Stir the paste into the remaining olive oil in a jar or bottle and refrigerate. The oil will be ready in a few days and will keep up to 3 weeks.

# Index

vinaigrette, radish and cucumber salad
with, 63
Chocolate:
cake, melting, 220
cakes, individual red banana, 218–219
and rum torte, 204–205
sauce, 208
*see also* White chocolate
Cilantro, 8
Cingolani, Dick, 22
Cinnamon:
bananas, sautéed, 200
brown rice, 85
ice cream, 199
Citron mousse, 210–211
Citrus:
and chili salsa, sautéed salmon with,
102–103
-roasted salmon, 99
Citrus-banana vinaigrette, 30
sliced duck breast with, 29–30
Clafoutis, black cherry, 209
Clams, littleneck, spaghettini with, 79
Cobbler, pear, apple, and black cherry,
214–215
Coconut:
curry sauce, shrimp taco with, 22–23
ice cream, 219
sole, with orange-lime sauce, 97
Compote:
mango, 205
papaya-pineapple, grilled yellowfin tuna
with, 118–119
Corn(meal):
goat cheese polenta, 92
grilled, and red pepper vinaigrette,
chicken salad with, 68–69
grilled, black beans, and tomato relish,
180–181
grilled, custard, 182–183
and wild mushroom fricassee, 19
Couscous and pork tenderloin salad, 70–
71
Crab(meat):
blue, cakes with mango and papaya
sauce, 120–121
crepes, 27–28
Crème brûlée, raspberry, 212–213
Crème fraîche, 9
chive, 241
Crepes, crabmeat, 27–28
Crisp, strawberry, papaya, and banana, 216
Crostini:
garlic, 31

mozzarella, tomato, and basil, 32
prosciutto, leek, and goat cheese, 33
Croutons, Fontina, Left Bank Caesar salad
with, 56–57
Cucumber(s):
European or English, 39, 116
and mint sauce, pan-seared tuna with,
116–117
and radish salad, with chive vinaigrette,
63
Cumin and sunflower seeds vinaigrette,
grilled lamb chops with, 150–151
Curry(ied):
coconut sauce, shrimp taco with, 22–
23
endive salad, 59
Custard:
grilled corn, 182–183
raspberry crème brûlée, 212–213
roasted shallot flan, 188

Dairy products, 9
Daube provençale, 161–162
Desserts, 195–226
black cherry clafoutis, 209
black-peppered strawberries, 223
chocolate and rum torte, 204–205
chocolate sauce, 208
citron mousse, 210–211
mango compote, 205
maple and almond zabaglione with
mixed berries, 201
pear, apple, and black cherry cobbler,
214–215
raspberry coulis, 211
raspberry crème brûlée, 212–213
sautéed cinnamon bananas, 200
strawberry, papaya, and banana crisp,
216
vanilla-orange blossom sauce, 221
*see also* Cake; Ice cream; Tart
Dill:
carrot, and ginger soup, 45
and grapefruit vinaigrette, 112, 113
Duck, 136–143
black cherry, pearl onion, and kirsch
sauce for, 141
breast, grilled, with olive and chili
sauce, 136–137
breast, sliced, with banana-citrus
vinaigrette, 29–30
roast, honey-glazed, 142–143

Duck (*cont.*)
   roast, with prune and mango sauce,
      138–140
   stock, 235

Eggplant, grilled, and roasted red peppers,
   55
Eggs, 9
Endive salad, curried, 59
Equipment, notes on, 11–12

Fettuccine:
   black, with Florida lobster, 83
   with shrimp provençale, 82
Filet mignon, roasted, with shallot, Pinot
      Noir, and pistachio sauce, 163
Fish, 95–122
   coconut sole with orange-lime sauce, 97
   pan-seared monkfish with saffron aioli,
      100–101
   sautéed halibut with aromatic
      vegetables, 98
   *see also* Mahi-mahi; Red snapper;
      Salmon; Swordfish; Tuna
Flan, roasted shallot, 188
Fleur de Lys (San Francisco), 37
Fontina croutons, Left Bank Caesar salad
      with, 56–57

Garlic, 10
   and basil basmati rice, 86
   blanching of, 20
   and chunky tomato sauce, roasted
      swordfish with, 114–115
   crostini, 31
   -herb cheese, roasted free-range chicken
      stuffed with, 126–127
   oil, roasted, 247
   and onion-roasted potatoes, 191
   roasted rosemary, 190
   and scallion soup, 47
Gazpacho, yellow pepper and tomato, 38–39
Ginger(ed):
   and beet soup, chilled, 37
   carrot, and dill soup, 45
   and carrot juice, risotto with, 88–89
   chicken breasts, 130–131
   and lime sauce, chicken breasts with,
      130–131

   and lime sauce, sautéed mahi-mahi with,
      110–111
   and mustard sauce, nut-crusted red
      snapper in, 108
Glaze(d):
   carrots, 179
   honey, for roast duck, 142, 143
   mustard, for roast chicken, 131
Goat cheese, 9
   polenta, 92
   prosciutto, and leek crostini, 33
   ravioli, with port wine sauce, 76–77
Grand Marnier–kumquat jam, 224–225
Grapefruit and dill vinaigrette, 112, 113
Grape-seed oil, 7
   arugula, 244
   chive, 244
Green beans with Calamata olives and
      toasted pine nuts, 177
Greens, mixed, sesame-crusted tuna on, 67
Gressette, Felicia, 62
Grilled dishes:
   chicken breast with Calamata olive
      sauce, 135
   chicken breast with papaya and avocado
      sauce, 129
   chicken salad with chili mayonnaise, 69
   corn, black beans, and tomato relish,
      180–181
   corn and red pepper vinaigrette, chicken
      salad with, 68–69
   corn custard, 182–183
   duck breast with olive and chili sauce,
      136–137
   eggplant and roasted red peppers, 55
   lamb chops with sunflower seeds and
      cumin vinaigrette, 150–151
   mahi-mahi with avocado salsa, 109
   Oriental swordfish with three-bean
      relish, 115
   pork chops on onion and bell pepper
      relish, 158–159
   salmon with pink peppercorn sauce, 103
   scallops with yellow bell pepper–black
      bean salsa, 24–25
   shrimp with chervil butter sauce, 20–21
   steak chimichurri, 165
   yellowfin tuna with papaya-pineapple
      compote, 118–119

Halibut, sautéed, with aromatic vegetables,
   98

Mesclun salad, 67
Mint and cucumber sauce, pan-seared tuna
    with, 116–117
Monkfish, pan-seared with saffron aioli,
    100–101
Moulin, Michel, 3
Mousse, citron, 210–211
Mozzarella, 9
    tomato, and basil crostini, 32
Mushroom(s):
    shiitake, roasted veal loin with, 168
    and Vidalia onion salad, 62
    wild, and corn fricassee, 19
    wild, turkey breast with, 144–145
Mustard:
    and ginger sauce, nut-crusted red
        snapper in, 108
    -glazed roast chicken, 131

New potatoes and beet salad, with scallion
    vinaigrette, 60–61
Niçoise vinaigrette, sautéed chicken breast
    with, 132–133
Nut(s):
    banana macadamia cake with maple
        sauce, 202–203
    -crusted red snapper in mustard and
        ginger sauce, 108
    roasted filet mignon with shallot, Pinot
        Noir, and pistachio sauce, 163
    toasted pine, green beans with Calamata
        olives and, 177
    see also Almond

Oils, 6–7
    flavored, 243–247
    fresh herb, 243
    see also Grape-seed oil; Olive oil
Olive(s), 10
    Calamata, green beans with toasted pine
        nuts and, 177
    Calamata, penne with, 75
    Calamata, sauce, grilled chicken breast
        with, 135
    Calamata, tapenade, roasted New York
        steak with, 164
    and chili sauce, grilled duck breast with,
        136–137
    green, shrimp, and tomato sauce,
        linguine with, 80–81

Olive oil, 6
    black, 244
    dried chili, 245
    roasted garlic, 247
Onion(s):
    and bell pepper relish, grilled pork
        chops on, 158–159
    caramelized, roasted pork chops with,
        156–157
    and garlic-roasted potatoes, 191
    pearl, black cherry, and kirsch sauce,
        141
    Vidalia, and mushroom salad, 62
Orange:
    blossom–vanilla sauce, 221
    -glazed pork tenderloin, 160
    -lime sauce, coconut sole with, 97
Oriental swordfish, grilled, with three-bean
    relish, 115
Osso buco provençale, 170–171

Pancetta salsa, sautéed red snapper with,
    104–105
Pan-seared tuna with cucumber and mint
    sauce, 116–117
Pan-seared veal chops with lime and
    scallions, 169
Pan-steamed monkfish, with saffron aioli,
    100–101
Papaya(s), 10
    and avocado sauce, grilled chicken
        breast with, 129
    beurre blanc, Sunshine red snapper
        with, 106–107
    crème brûlée, 213
    and mango sauce, blue crab cakes with,
        120–121
    -pineapple compote, grilled yellowfin
        tuna with, 118–119
    strawberry, and banana crisp, 216
Parisienne potatoes, 192–193
Parmesan cheese, 9
Pasta, 1, 73–84
    black fettuccine with Florida lobster, 83
    fettuccine with shrimp provençale, 82
    goat cheese ravioli with port wine sauce,
        76–77
    linguine with shrimp, green olive, and
        tomato sauce, 80–81
    penne with Calamata olives, 75
    rigatoni and herbed chicken strips, 84
    spaghettini with littleneck clams, 79

Relish (*cont.*)
onion and bell pepper, grilled pork
chops on, 158–159
Relish, three-bean, 186–187
grilled Oriental swordfish with, 115
Rice, 85–91
with chicken (arroz con pollo), 125
cinnamon brown, 85
garlic and basil basmati, 86
*see also* Risotto
Rice wine vinegar, 7
Rigatoni and herbed chicken strips, 84
Risotto:
with ginger and carrot juice, 88–89
saffron, 87
seafood, with tomato and basil juice, 90–
91
Roast(ed)
butternut squash and sherry bisque, 42–
43
chicken breasts with red bell pepper
sauce, 128
duck with prune and mango sauce, 138–
139
filet mignon with shallot, Pinot Noir, and
pistachio sauce, 163
free-range chicken stuffed with garlic-
herb cheese, 126–127
garlic oil, 247
New York steak with Calamata olive
tapenade, 164
peppers and chili sabayon sauce, 134
pork chops with caramelized onions,
156–157
pork loin with aromatic vegetables, 152–
153
rosemary garlic, 190
shallot flan, 188
shallot vinaigrette, leek salad with, 58–
59
swordfish with chunky tomato and
garlic sauce, 114–115
veal chops with green peppercorn
sauce, 166–167
veal loin with shiitake mushrooms, 168
Rosemary garlic, roasted, 190
Rum and chocolate torte, 204–205


Sabayon sauce, roasted peppers and chili,
134
Saffron:
aioli, pan-served monkfish with, 100–101

risotto, 87
substitute for, 125
Salads, 53–72
aioli shrimp, 65
chicken, grilled, with chili mayonnaise,
69
chicken, with red pepper and grilled
corn vinaigrette, 68–69
curried endive, 59
grilled eggplant and roasted red
peppers, 55
leek, with roasted shallot vinaigrette,
58–59
Left Bank Caesar, with Fontina
croutons, 56–57
lime scallop, 66
mushroom and Vidalia onion, 62
new potatoes and beet, with scallion
vinaigrette, 60–61
pork tenderloin and couscous, 70–71
radish and cucumber, with chive
vinaigrette, 63
sesame-crusted tuna on mixed greens,
67
vine-ripened tomato, with sweet basil
vinaigrette, 64
Salmon:
citrus-roasted, 99
grilled, with pink peppercorn sauce, 103
sautéed, with citrus and chili salsa, 102–
103
Salsa:
avocado, grilled mahi-mahi with, 109
citrus and chili, sautéed salmon with,
102–103
pancetta, sautéed red snapper with, 104–
105
shrimp, 23
yellow bell pepper–black bean, grilled
scallops with, 24–25
Sauce(s):
black cherry, pearl onion, and kirsch,
141
Calamata olive, grilled chicken breast
with, 135
chervil butter, grilled shrimp with, 20–21
chocolate, 208
chunky tomato and garlic, roasted
swordfish with, 114–115
coconut curry, shrimp taco with, 22–23
cucumber and mint, pan-seared tuna
with, 116–117
ginger and lime, chicken breasts with,
130–131